KT-405-244

EDITOR: Maryanne Blacker

FOOD EDITOR: Pamela Clark

• • •

DESIGNER: Louise McGeachie

• • •

ASSISTANT FOOD EDITORS:
Jan Castorina, Karen Green

ASSOCIATE FOOD EDITOR:
Enid Morrison

CHIEF HOME ECONOMIST: Kathy Wharton

DEPUTY CHIEF HOME ECONOMIST:
Louise Patniotis

HOME ECONOMISTS: Tracey Kern, Quinton Kohler,
Jill Lange, Alexandra McCowan, Kathy McGarry,
Kathy Snowball, Dimitra Stais

EDITORIAL COORDINATOR: Elizabeth Hooper

KITCHEN ASSISTANT: Amy Wong

• • •

STYLISTS: Marie-Helene Clauzon, Rosemary de Santis,
Michelle Gorry, Jacqui Hing, Anna Phillips

PHOTOGRAPHERS: Bruce Allan, Kevin Brown,
Robert Clark, Andre Martin, Robert Taylor, Jon Waddy

• • •

HOME LIBRARY STAFF:

ASSISTANT EDITOR: Beverley Hudec

DESIGNER: Paula Wooller

• • •

ACP PUBLISHER: Richard Walsh

ACP ASSOCIATE PUBLISHER: Bob Neil

• • •

Produced by The Australian Women's Weekly Home Library.
Typeset by ACP Colour Graphics Pty Ltd. Printed by Dai
Nippon Co., Ltd in Japan.
Published by ACP Publishing, 54 Park Street Sydney.
◆ AUSTRALIA: Distributed by Network Distribution Company,
54 Park Street Sydney, (02) 282 8777.
◆ NEW ZEALAND: Distributed in New Zealand by Netlink
Distribution Company, 17B Hargreaves St, Level 5,
College Hill, Auckland 1 (9) 302 7616.
◆ UNITED KINGDOM: Distributed in the U.K. by ACP
Publishing (UK) Ltd, 20 Galowhill Rd, Brackmills,
Northampton NN4 0EE (0604) 760 456.
◆ CANADA: Distributed in Canada by Whitecap Books Ltd,
1086 West 3rd St,
North Vancouver V7P 3J6 (604) 9809852.
◆ SOUTH AFRICA: Distributed in South Africa by Intermag,
PO Box 57394, Springfield 2137 (011) 4933200.
ACN 053 273 546

• • •

Finger Food

Includes index.
ISBN 0 949128 26 0.

1. Cookery. 2. Snack foods.
(Series : Australian Women's Weekly
Home Library).

641.53

• • •

© A C P Publishing

This publication is copyright. No part of it may be reproduced
or transmitted in any form without the written permission
of the publishers.
First published 1990. Reprinted 1991, 1992

COVER: Clockwise from left: Chicken Drummettes in Crisp
Spicy Batter, Peppery Cheese Puffs, Smoked Fish
Vol-au-Vents, page 9.
OPPOSITE: Crisp Little Potato Rosti with Lemon
Chive Cream, page 26.
BACK COVER: From front: Cucumber Rounds with
Herbed Cream Cheese, Roast Beef and Avocado
on Pumpernickel, page 77.

FINGER FOOD

Here are around 200 tempting recipes, hot and cold,
for the best party food ever! Some are easy
some more elaborate, so you can mix and match to suit
everything from a cocktail party through to a family barbecue.
On the next page you'll find helpful party planning tips,
then each recipe has do ahead, storage and freezing hints
to help you even more. By "prepared", we mean
up to the stage before cooking or completing. By "made",
we mean ready to serve or assemble.

Pamela Clark

FOOD EDITOR

BRITISH & NORTH AMERICAN READERS: Please note that Australian cup
and spoon measurements are metric. Conversion charts for cup and spoon
measurements and oven temperatures appear on page 124.
A glossary explaining unfamiliar terms and ingredients appears on page 122.

Hot Savouries

Our instructions for doing ahead will save you time and stress. You'll know how to plan your party if you know what to do in advance. Some recipes can be prepared beforehand, others can be completed and reheated. To reheat savouries, place in single layer on oven trays, cover loosely with foil, slash holes in the foil about 5cm apart, then heat in moderate oven, unless otherwise specified.

PARTY PLANNING

A party at home is more fun if you are well organised. Planning is the key. Devise a selection of finger food that suits your guests' tastes and your budget, then make lots of lists.

Foodwise, make two shopping lists (one with items to buy ahead; the other with last-minute "perishables"), then plan your cooking timetable, starting with recipes that are suitable to freeze.
Take stock of "accessories", too. Have you enough serving plates and china, cutlery, tables, chairs, glasses, linen and so on? You may need trays if you plan to pass the finger food around.
Friends and relatives can often help with china, cutlery and glasses, but it may be more convenient to hire the things you need. Shop around before hiring; we found the variations in prices quite amazing.
To make things run more smoothly, consider hiring someone to serve and clean up. Many agencies provide these services and they are surprisingly inexpensive.

QUANTITIES: One of the most difficult decisions is how much food and drink you will need to supply. We have stated how many savouries are made from each recipe. As a general guide, allow 6 pieces per person for the first hour, and about another 4 pieces for each further hour. We like a variety of hot and cold savouries, depending on the season and the occasion. It's a good idea to take into consideration a mix of colours, tastes and textures. Young people tend to eat more, so serve extra crisps, crackers, nuts, pretzels, cheese and olives, etc.
To indicate the party is over, serve some lovely chocolates or petits fours with coffee where the occasion is suitable.

DRINKS: Drinks are even more difficult to estimate than food. You may wish to serve spirits or cocktails when guests arrive, or simply serve beer, wine (including sparkling and champagne style) and/or juice, mineral water and non-alcoholic drinks. Wine can be served throughout the party. It's helpful to put drinks in an accessible spot with someone to serve them.
Of course, don't forget the ice and plenty of serviettes!

DUCK AND SPINACH MINI PIZZAS

15g compressed yeast
½ teaspoon sugar
½ cup lukewarm water
1½ cups plain flour
2 tablespoons oil
¼ cup tomato paste
1 tablespoon oil, extra
1 clove garlic, crushed
2 duck breast fillets, sliced
½ bunch (20 leaves) English
    spinach, shredded
¾ cup grated fresh parmesan cheese

Cream yeast and sugar in bowl, stir in water, stand in warm place for about 10 minutes or until foamy.

Sift flour into bowl, stir in oil and yeast mixture, mix to a firm dough. Turn dough onto lightly floured surface, knead for about 10 minutes or until dough is smooth and elastic. Place dough in lightly oiled bowl; cover, stand in warm place for 30 minutes or until dough doubles in size.

Turn dough onto lightly floured surface, knead until smooth. Divide dough into quarters, divide each quarter into 10 pieces. Knead each piece into a smooth ball, press to flatten. Place rounds on lightly greased oven trays, spread lightly with tomato paste.

Heat extra oil in pan, add garlic, cook 1 minute. Add duck, cook, stirring, for about 2 minutes or until just browned; remove from pan. Add spinach to pan, cook, stirring, for about 1 minute or until soft. Spoon spinach onto pizzas, top with duck, sprinkle with cheese. Bake in hot oven for about 10 minutes or until cheese is melted and pizza base cooked through.
    Makes 40.
■ Pizzas can be made a day ahead, reheat in oven.
■ Storage: Covered, in refrigerator.
■ Freeze: Not suitable.
■ Microwave: Not suitable.

RIGHT: Duck and Spinach Mini Pizzas.

CURRIED VEGETABLE SAMOSAS

2 tablespoons oil
1 onion, chopped
1 clove garlic, crushed
2 teaspoons curry powder
1 large (200g) potato, finely chopped
1 small carrot, finely chopped
2 tablespoons frozen peas
5 sheets ready rolled
  shortcrust pastry
1 tablespoon milk
oil for deep-frying

Heat oil in pan, add onion, garlic and curry powder, cook, stirring, until onion is soft. Stir in potato and carrot, cook 5 minutes or until tender, stir in peas; cool.

Cut 8cm rounds from pastry. Top each round with 1 level teaspoon of potato mixture, brush edges with milk, fold in half, press edges together.

Just before serving, deep-fry samosas in hot oil until well browned.

Makes about 45.

■ Can be prepared 2 days ahead.
■ Storage: Covered, in refrigerator.
■ Freeze: Uncooked samosas suitable.
■ Microwave: Not suitable.

GLAZED CHICKEN BITES

500g minced chicken
1 egg, lightly beaten
½ teaspoon ground coriander
½ teaspoon five spice powder
2 teaspoons chopped fresh chives
½ cup stale breadcrumbs

GLAZE
½ cup redcurrant jelly
½ cup mango chutney
2 teaspoons lemon juice

Combine chicken, egg, spices, chives and breadcrumbs in bowl. Shape level tablespoons of mixture into balls, place on baking paper-lined oven tray. Bake in hot oven for about 15 minutes or until well browned; drain on absorbent paper.

Just before serving, add chicken bites to glaze in pan, simmer for about 3 minutes or until lightly glazed.

Glaze: Combine jelly, chutney and juice in pan, stir glaze mixture over medium heat until combined.

Makes about 40.

■ Bites can be prepared 2 days ahead.
■ Storage: Covered, in refrigerator.
■ Freeze: Suitable.
■ Microwave: Not suitable.

BACON MINI POTATOES

440g can baby new potatoes, drained
1 teaspoon French mustard
3 bacon rashers

Cut potatoes in halves, spread cut surfaces with a little mustard, trim a small piece from each rounded side to make level. Cut bacon into 2cm x 4cm strips, cover flat side of potatoes with bacon, secure with toothpicks.

Just before serving, grill until bacon is crisp and browned.

Makes about 20.

■ Can be prepared 2 days ahead.
■ Storage: Covered, in refrigerator.
■ Freeze: Not suitable.
■ Microwave: Suitable.

BELOW: From left: Curried Vegetable Samosas, Glazed Chicken Bites, Bacon Mini Potatoes.
RIGHT: From left: Mini Steamed Pork Buns, Pepper Camembert and Bacon Wontons.

Below: China from J.D. Milner

MINI STEAMED PORK BUNS

15g dry yeast
1 cup warm water
½ cup castor sugar
2 cups plain flour
1 cup self-raising flour
30g lard, melted
FILLING
1 tablespoon oil
3 green shallots, chopped
1 teaspoon grated fresh ginger
2 teaspoons cornflour
¼ cup water
1 tablespoon light soy sauce
2 teaspoons hoisin sauce
1 teaspoon sugar
1 tablespoon dry sherry
250g Chinese barbecued
** pork, chopped**

Combine yeast, ⅓ cup of the water and 2 teaspoons of the sugar in small bowl. Sprinkle with 2 teaspoons of the plain flour; cover, stand in warm place for about 10 minutes or until frothy.

Combine remaining sugar and sifted flours in large bowl, stir in remaining water, lard and yeast mixture, mix to a soft dough. Turn dough onto floured surface, knead for 10 minutes or until dough is smooth and elastic. Place in lightly oiled bowl; cover, stand in warm place for about 1 hour or until dough is doubled in size.

Knead dough until smooth, divide into 48 pieces. Knead each piece into a ball, flatten each ball, place 1 level teaspoon of filling on centre of each ball. Gather edges to enclose filling, pinch together to seal, place pinched side down on 3cm squares of greaseproof paper. Place buns about 3cm apart in steamer; cover, cook over boiling water for about 10 minutes or until buns are dry to touch. Remove paper before serving.

Filling: Heat oil in pan, add shallots and ginger, stir over heat 1 minute. Stir in blended cornflour and water, then sauces, sugar, sherry and pork. Stir over heat until mixture boils and thickens, remove from heat; cool.

Makes 48.

■ Buns can be made a day ahead, reheat in steamer for 4 minutes.
■ Storage: Covered, in refrigerator.
■ Freeze: Cooked buns suitable.
■ Microwave: Not suitable.

PEPPER CAMEMBERT AND BACON WONTONS

4 bacon rashers, finely chopped
125g pepper camembert cheese,
** finely chopped**
24 egg pastry sheets
1 egg white, lightly beaten
oil for deep-frying

Cook bacon in pan, stirring, until crisp; drain on absorbent paper. Place level teaspoons each of bacon and cheese on centre of each pastry sheet, brush edges lightly with egg white. Fold sheets in half diagonally, press edges to seal. Brush 2 opposite points lightly with egg white, pinch together.

Just before serving, deep-fry wontons in hot oil until puffed and well browned; drain on absorbent paper. Serve hot.

Makes about 24.

■ Wontons can be prepared a day ahead.
■ Storage: Covered, in refrigerator.
■ Freeze: Uncooked wontons suitable.
■ Microwave: Not suitable.

GRUYERE AND PECAN PASTRY PARCELS

125g gruyere cheese, chopped
100g ricotta cheese
1 stick celery, finely chopped
½ teaspoon chopped fresh rosemary
1 egg, lightly beaten
pinch cayenne pepper
2 tablespoons chopped pecans
6 sheets fillo pastry
60g butter, melted

Combine cheeses, celery, rosemary, egg, pepper and nuts in bowl; mix well.

Brush 3 sheets of pastry with some of the butter; layer together. Cut sheets into 8cm squares, top each square with a level teaspoon of cheese mixture, bring corners together in centre, press edges together firmly. Repeat with remaining pastry, butter and filling. Place parcels on lightly greased oven trays, brush lightly with butter; cover, refrigerate 1 hour.

Just before serving, bake in moderately hot oven for about 15 minutes or until browned and crisp.

Makes about 36.
■ Parcels can be prepared a day ahead.
■ Storage: Covered, in refrigerator.
■ Freeze: Uncooked parcels suitable.
■ Microwave: Not suitable.

OLIVE AND SUN-DRIED TOMATO TARTLETS

½ cup wholemeal plain flour
½ cup white plain flour
½ teaspoon paprika
30g butter
¼ cup grated fresh parmesan cheese
2 tablespoons water, approximately
2 tablespoons grated fresh parmesan cheese, extra

OLIVE AND TOMATO FILLING
1 tablespoon olive oil
1 onion, chopped
1 clove garlic, crushed
1 small zucchini, chopped
⅓ cup chopped sun-dried tomatoes
⅓ cup pitted chopped black olives
2 tablespoons chopped fresh basil

Sift dry ingredients into bowl, rub in butter, stir in cheese and enough water to make ingredients cling together. Knead on lightly floured surface until dough is smooth; cover, refrigerate 30 minutes.

Roll dough between sheets of greaseproof paper until 1mm thick. Cut 5cm rounds from dough, place rounds in 4½cm tart pans, prick pastry all over with fork. Bake in moderate oven for about 15 minutes or until lightly browned; cool.

Just before serving, spoon mixture into pastry cases, sprinkle with extra cheese, bake in moderate oven for about 5 minutes or until heated through.

Olive and Tomato Filling: Heat oil in pan, add onion, garlic and zucchini, cook, stirring, for about 3 minutes or until onion is soft; remove from heat. Stir in tomatoes, olives and basil.

Makes about 40.
■ Pastry cases can be cooked and filling prepared 2 days ahead.
■ Storage: Pastry cases in airtight container. Filling, covered, in refrigerator.
■ Freeze: Pastry cases suitable.
■ Microwave: Filling suitable.

LEFT: Gruyere and Pecan Pastry Parcels.
BELOW: Olive and Sun-Dried Tomato Tartlets.

Left: Platter from Villeroy & Boch. Below: Plate from Mosmania

CHICKEN DRUMMETTES IN CRISP SPICY BATTER

12 (about 1kg) chicken wings
2 tablespoons besan flour
¼ cup self-raising flour
½ teaspoon chilli powder
½ teaspoon garam masala
¼ teaspoon ground cumin
¼ teaspoon ground coriander
½ cup water
oil for deep-frying
SAUCE
½ cup Chinese barbecue sauce
¼ cup water
½ teaspoon chopped fresh chillies

Cut first and second joints from wings. Holding small end of third joint; trim around bone with sharp knife. Cut, scrape and push meat down to large end. Pull skin and meat down over ends of bones; they will resemble baby drumsticks.

Sift dry ingredients into bowl, gradually stir in water.

Just before serving, dip drummettes into batter, deep-fry in hot oil until lightly browned and cooked through. Serve hot with sauce.

Sauce: Combine sauce, water and chillies in pan, bring to boil.

Makes 12.
■ Wings can be trimmed 2 days ahead. Batter can be prepared 3 hours ahead.
■ Storage: Covered, in refrigerator.
■ Freeze: Uncooked wings suitable.
■ Microwave: Sauce suitable.

SMOKED FISH AND HERB VOL-AU-VENTS

100g smoked cod, skinned, boned
2 egg yolks
1 tablespoon mayonnaise
1 tablespoon chopped fresh chives
1 tablespoon chopped fresh parsley
½ teaspoon French mustard
¼ cup grated tasty cheese
1 egg white
2 x 60g packets oyster cases

Blend or process cod, egg yolks and mayonnaise until smooth. Transfer mixture to bowl, stir in herbs, mustard and cheese; mix well.

Just before serving, beat egg white in bowl until soft peaks form, fold into fish mixture. Spoon mixture into oyster cases, place on oven trays. Bake vol-au-vents in moderate oven for about 10 minutes or until lightly browned.

Makes 24.
■ Filling can be made 3 hours ahead.
■ Storage: Covered, in refrigerator.
■ Freeze: Not suitable.
■ Microwave: Not suitable.

LEFT: Clockwise from left: Chicken Drummettes in Crisp Spicy Batter, Peppery Cheese Puffs, Smoked Fish and Herb Vol-au-Vents.
China from Kenwick Galleries

PEPPERY CHEESE PUFFS

1 cup water
80g butter
1 cup plain flour
1 teaspoon seasoned pepper
3 eggs, lightly beaten
¾ cup (100g) grated tasty cheese
¼ cup grated fresh parmesan cheese
oil for deep-frying

Combine water and butter in pan, bring to boil, stirring, until butter is melted. Add flour and pepper all at once. Stir vigorously over medium heat until mixture leaves the side of pan and forms a smooth ball. Place mixture in small bowl of electric mixer (or in processor). Add eggs gradually, beating on low speed after each addition. Fold in cheeses; mix well.

Just before serving, deep-fry rounded teaspoons of mixture in hot oil until lightly browned and cooked through. Drain on absorbent paper.

Makes about 60.
■ Mixture can be prepared 3 hours ahead.
■ Storage: At room temperature.
■ Freeze: Not suitable.
■ Microwave: Not suitable.

MINI ROTI WITH SPICY TOMATO SAUCE

1 cup plain flour
2 green shallots, chopped
¾ cup boiling water, approximately

SPICY TOMATO SAUCE
10g butter
2 cloves garlic, crushed
¼ teaspoon grated fresh ginger
1 teaspoon ground coriander
½ teaspoon ground cumin
pinch chilli powder
½ teaspoon turmeric
½ x 300g can Tomato Supreme
¼ cup water

Sift flour into bowl, stir in shallots, quickly stir in enough boiling water to mix to a soft dough. Turn onto floured surface, knead until smooth. Roll 2 level teaspoons of dough into a thin sausage about 15cm long. Repeat with remaining dough. Coil sausages, flatten between hands.

Roll flattened coils on floured surface into rounds about 8cm in diameter. Cook rounds in lightly greased heavy-based pan, pressing flat with large spoon while cooking, until lightly browned on both sides. Serve roti hot with hot sauce.

Spicy Tomato Sauce: Heat butter in pan, add garlic and spices, cook for 2 minutes over medium heat. Stir in Tomato Supreme and water, bring to boil, simmer, uncovered, for about 8 minutes or until sauce is thickened.

Makes about 30.
- ■ Roti can be prepared several hours ahead; reheat in oven. Sauce can be made 2 days ahead.
- ■ Storage: Roti, covered, at room temperature. Sauce, covered, in refrigerator.
- ■ Freeze: Not suitable.
- ■ Microwave: Sauce suitable.

APRICOT CHICKEN TRIANGLES

1 tablespoon oil
1 small onion, finely chopped
500g minced chicken
⅓ cup finely chopped dried apricots
½ teaspoon ground cumin
pinch chilli powder
1 loaf sliced white bread
1 egg, lightly beaten
oil for deep-frying

Heat oil in pan, add onion, cook, stirring, until onion is soft. Stir in chicken, apricots, cumin and chilli; cook, stirring, for 5 minutes; cool.

Remove crusts from bread, roll each slice with rolling pin until thin. Cut slices in halves diagonally. Lightly brush triangles with egg, top each triangle with ¼ level teaspoon of filling. Fold triangles in halves, press edges together with a fork.

Just before serving, deep-fry triangles until browned; drain on absorbent paper.

Makes about 40.
- ■ Triangles can be prepared for cooking 2 hours ahead.
- ■ Storage: Covered, in refrigerator.
- ■ Freeze: Uncooked triangles suitable.
- ■ Microwave: Not suitable.

*BELOW: Mini Roti with Spicy Tomato Sauce.
RIGHT: From left: Apricot Chicken Triangles, Corn Puffs with Lemon Chilli Sauce.*

Below: Indian sari from The Caspian Studio. Right: Basket and terracotta ware from Barbara's House & Garden

CORN PUFFS WITH LEMON CHILLI SAUCE

1 cup cornmeal
1 green shallot, finely chopped
½ cup stale breadcrumbs
½ cup self-raising flour
¼ teaspoon baking powder
1 teaspoon sugar
1 egg, lightly beaten
2 tablespoons taco sauce
½ small red pepper, finely chopped
¾ cup water, approximately
oil for deep-frying

LEMON CHILLI SAUCE
2 tablespoons lemon spread
1 tablespoon taco sauce
⅓ cup water

Combine cornmeal, shallot, breadcrumbs and sifted dry ingredients in bowl, gradually stir in egg, sauce, pepper and enough water to make a stiff mixture.
Just before serving, deep-fry level tablespoons of mixture in hot oil until lightly browned and cooked through; drain on absorbent paper. Serve puffs hot with warm sauce.

Lemon Chilli Sauce: Combine all ingredients in pan, bring to boil.
Makes about 25.
■ Mixture can be prepared 3 hours ahead. Sauce can be made 2 days ahead.
■ Storage: At room temperature.
■ Freeze: Not suitable.
■ Microwave: Sauce suitable.

PARMESAN BASIL FRANKFURTS

3 frankfurts
plain flour
2 eggs, lightly beaten
1¼ cups (100g) grated fresh
    parmesan cheese
2 tablespoons chopped fresh parsley
2 tablespoons chopped fresh basil
2 teaspoons ground black pepper
oil for deep-frying
TOMATO BASIL SAUCE
1 tablespoon olive oil
1 onion, finely chopped
2 cloves garlic, crushed
440g can tomatoes
1 cup water
2 teaspoons sweet sherry
2 tablespoons chopped fresh basil
1 tablespoon chopped fresh parsley

Cut frankfurts diagonally into 1cm slices. Toss slices in flour, shake away excess flour, dip into eggs, then into combined cheese, parsley, basil and pepper. Press cheese mixture firmly onto frankfurt slices; cover, refrigerate 15 minutes.
Just before serving, deep-fry frankfurt slices in hot oil until lightly browned; drain on absorbent paper. Serve hot with sauce.
Tomato Basil Sauce: Heat oil in pan, add onion and garlic, cook, stirring, until onion is soft. Stir in undrained crushed tomatoes, water and sherry, bring to boil, simmer, uncovered, for about 20 minutes or until thickened; stir in herbs.
    Makes about 40.
■ Frankfurts can be prepared 2 days ahead.
■ Storage: Covered, in refrigerator.
■ Freeze: Suitable.
■ Microwave: Sauce suitable.

MINI CURRIED EGG PUFFS

3 sheets ready rolled puff pastry
4 hard-boiled eggs
2 teaspoons curry powder
2 tablespoons mayonnaise
1 tablespoon chopped fresh chives
1 egg, lightly beaten
1 teaspoon poppy seeds

Cut 8cm rounds from pastry. Mash hard-boiled eggs, curry powder, mayonnaise and chives with a fork in bowl. Place 2 level teaspoons of mixture together in centre of each pastry round. Lightly brush edges of rounds with egg, fold rounds in half, press edges together.
    Place puffs on lightly greased oven trays, brush lightly with egg, sprinkle lightly with poppy seeds.
Just before serving, bake puffs in moderately hot oven for about 12 minutes or until well browned.
    Makes 27.
■ Puffs can be prepared a day ahead.
■ Storage: Covered, in refrigerator.
■ Freeze: Not suitable.
■ Microwave: Not suitable.

SPICED APPLE MEATBALLS

500g minced beef
1 small onion, finely chopped
½ cup finely chopped dried apple
1 green shallot, finely chopped
2 tablespoons chopped fresh parsley
1 tablespoon brandy
¼ teaspoon ground cinnamon
pinch ground nutmeg
2 tablespoons chopped
    pistachio nuts
1 egg
1 cup (100g) stale breadcrumbs
2 tablespoons oil

Combine mince, onion, apple, shallot, parsley, brandy, cinnamon, nutmeg, nuts and egg in bowl; mix well. Roll 2 level teaspoons of mixture into a ball then coat in breadcrumbs. Repeat with remaining mixture and breadcrumbs. Heat oil in pan, add meatballs, cook until browned all over and cooked through. Serve hot.
    Makes about 50.
■ Meatballs can be made 2 days ahead.
■ Storage: Covered, in refrigerator.
■ Freeze: Suitable.
■ Microwave: Not suitable.

LEFT: From left: Parmesan Basil Frankfurts, Spiced Apple Meatballs, Mini Curried Egg Puffs.

Plates from Interim

CREAMY SCRAMBLED EGGS IN FLAKY PASTRY CASES

2 x 60g packets oyster cases
5 eggs
40g butter
30g ham, chopped
1 tablespoon chopped fresh parsley
1 tablespoon cream

Place oyster cases on oven tray. Lightly beat eggs in bowl until combined. Heat butter in pan, add eggs, stir gently over heat until beginning to set; remove from heat. Stir in ham, parsley and cream. Spoon mixture into oyster cases, keep warm in slow oven.

Makes 24.

■ Cases can be made 20 minutes ahead.
■ Storage: Not suitable.
■ Freeze: Not suitable.
■ Microwave: Not suitable.

ABOVE: From back: Creamy Scrambled Eggs in Flaky Pastry Cases, Seafood Bites with Lemon Ginger Sauce.
RIGHT: Seafood Rolls with Lemon Sauce.

Above: Plates from Villeroy and Boch; tiles from Country Floors. Right: Plate from Corso de Fiori

14

SEAFOOD BITES WITH LEMON GINGER SAUCE

250g uncooked prawns, shelled
250g scallops
250g boneless white fish fillets
1 egg
½ teaspoon grated lemon rind
2 tablespoons lemon juice
¼ cup chopped fresh parsley
oil for deep-frying
SAUCE
1 tablespoon cornflour
¼ cup lemon juice
¾ cup water
1 small chicken stock cube, crumbled
1 tablespoon honey
1 tablespoon brown sugar
1 teaspoon grated fresh ginger

Blend or process seafood, egg, rind, juice and parsley until well combined.

Just before serving, deep-fry rounded teaspoons of mixture in hot oil until well browned; drain on absorbent paper. Serve warm bites with warm sauce.

Sauce: Blend cornflour with juice in pan, stir in remaining ingredients, stir over heat until sauce boils and thickens.

Makes about 50.

■ Fish mixture can be made a day ahead.
■ Storage: Covered, in refrigerator.
■ Freeze: Not suitable.
■ Microwave: Not suitable.

SEAFOOD ROLLS WITH LEMON SAUCE

2 egg whites, lightly beaten
5 seafood sticks, finely chopped
170g can crab, drained
1 teaspoon lemon pepper
4 green shallots, chopped
15 sheets (17cm diameter)
    Thai rice paper
LEMON SAUCE
1 cup water
½ small chicken stock cube,
    crumbled
½ teaspoon grated lemon rind
½ cup lemon juice
pinch chilli powder
2 teaspoons cornflour
1 tablespoon water, extra
1 teaspoon chopped fresh chives

Combine egg whites, seafood, pepper and shallots in bowl.

Soak rice paper sheets in water for about 1 minute or until soft; drain. Cut

sheets in halves, place onto clean cloth. Top each half with 2 level teaspoons of seafood mixture, fold in long sides, then roll up from narrow ends.

Just before serving, place rolls in steamer in single layer, cook, covered, over simmering water until heated through. Serve hot with hot sauce.

Lemon Sauce: Combine water, stock cube, rind, juice and chilli in pan, stir over heat until mixture boils. Stir in blended cornflour and extra water, stir until mixture boils and thickens. Stir in chives just before serving.

Makes 30.

■ Rolls can be prepared 3 hours ahead.
■ Storage: Covered, in refrigerator.
■ Freeze: Not suitable.
■ Microwave: Not suitable.

Place oysters in ovenproof dish. Heat butter in pan, add shallots and garlic, cook, stirring, until shallots are soft, stir in herbs. Spoon over oysters, sprinkle with cheese. **Just before serving,** bake oysters in moderate oven for about 5 minutes or until heated through.

Makes 24.
- Oysters can be prepared a day ahead.
- Storage: Covered, in refrigerator.
- Freeze: Not suitable.
- Microwave: Suitable.

LEMON GINGER PRAWNS

30 (about 1kg) uncooked king prawns
2 teaspoons lemon juice
2 teaspoons grated fresh ginger
1 tablespoon light soy sauce
1 teaspoon sesame oil
pinch five spice powder
2 tablespoons oil

Shell and devein prawns, leaving tails intact. Combine juice, ginger, sauce, sesame oil and spice in bowl, stir in prawns; cover, refrigerate 1 hour.

Thread prawns onto 15 skewers.
Just before serving, heat oil in pan, add skewers, cook until tender.

Makes 15.
- Prawns can be prepared a day ahead.
- Storage: Covered, in refrigerator.
- Freeze: Suitable.
- Microwave: Not suitable.

GARLIC AND PEPPER QUAIL BREASTS

24 quail breast fillets, halved
4 cloves garlic, crushed
1½ teaspoons cracked black
  peppercorns
1 tablespoon oil
1 tablespoon oil, extra

Combine quail, garlic, pepper and oil in bowl; cover, refrigerate 1 hour.
Just before serving, heat extra oil in pan, add quail, cook for about 2 minutes on each side or until well browned and tender. Serve immediately.

Makes 48.
- Quail can be prepared 2 days ahead.
- Storage: Covered, in refrigerator.
- Freeze: Suitable.
- Microwave: Not suitable.

SESAME CHEESE CROQUETTES

2 eggs
2 cups (250g) grated processed
  cheddar cheese
⅔ cup grated fresh parmesan cheese
2 tablespoons plain flour
¼ cup sesame seeds
1 tablespoon chopped fresh chives
2 tablespoons sesame seeds, extra
oil for deep-frying

Blend or process eggs, cheeses, flour, seeds and chives until combined; cover, refrigerate 30 minutes. Roll 2 level teaspoons of mixture into a croquette, roll

CRISPY CHICKEN KEBABS WITH SHERRIED CHILLI SAUCE

500g chicken thigh fillets
2 teaspoons grated fresh ginger
¼ cup light soy sauce
2 tablespoons dry sherry
cornflour
oil for shallow-frying

SHERRIED CHILLI SAUCE
¼ cup light soy sauce
2 teaspoons dry sherry
1 small fresh red chilli, sliced
1 clove garlic, sliced

Cut chicken into thin strips, thread onto 16 skewers. Using 2 spoons, squeeze juice from ginger, discard pulp. Combine ginger juice, sauce and sherry in bowl, pour over chicken; cover, stand 30 minutes.
Just before serving, toss kebabs in cornflour, shake away excess cornflour.

Shallow-fry kebabs in hot oil until chicken is crisp and tender. Serve hot with sauce.
Sherried Chilli Sauce: Combine all ingredients in bowl; mix well.

Makes 16.
- Unfloured kebabs can be prepared a day ahead.
- Storage: Covered, in refrigerator.
- Freeze: Unfloured kebabs suitable.
- Microwave: Not suitable.

BAKED OYSTERS WITH GARLIC HERB BUTTER

24 oysters in shells
60g butter
2 green shallots, chopped
1 clove garlic, crushed
2 teaspoons chopped fresh chives
1 teaspoon chopped fresh parsley
1 tablespoon grated fresh
  parmesan cheese

in extra seeds. Repeat with remaining mixture and extra seeds.

Just before serving, deep-fry croquettes in hot oil until well browned, drain on absorbent paper.

Makes about 40.

■ Can be prepared 2 days ahead.
■ Storage: Covered, in refrigerator.
■ Freeze: Not suitable.
■ Microwave: Not suitable.

ABOVE LEFT: From left: Crispy Chicken Kebabs with Sherried Chilli Sauce, Baked Oysters with Garlic Herb Butter.
ABOVE: From front: Lemon Ginger Prawns, Sesame Cheese Croquettes, Garlic and Pepper Quail Breasts.

Above left: Plates from Kenwick Galleries. Above: Platter from J.D.Milner

CURRIED CRESCENTS WITH TOMATO SAUCE

4½ cups self-raising flour
90g butter
1½ cups milk, approximately
1 egg, lightly beaten
oil for deep-frying

FILLING
1 tablespoon oil
1 clove garlic, crushed
1 small onion, chopped
300g pork and veal mince
2 tablespoons chopped fresh parsley
2 teaspoons curry powder
2 tablespoons tomato paste
1 tablespoon white vinegar
1 small red pepper, finely chopped
1 tablespoon plain flour
2 teaspoons water

TOMATO SAUCE
½ teaspoon oil
1 clove garlic, crushed
1 small onion, chopped
410g can tomatoes
1 tablespoon tomato paste
2 teaspoons sugar

Sift flour into bowl, rub in butter, stir in enough milk to mix to a firm dough. Knead dough gently on lightly floured surface until smooth. Roll dough on lightly floured surface until 3mm thick, cut into 5½cm rounds. Lightly brush rounds with egg, top each round with ¼ level teaspoon of filling. Fold rounds in half, press edges together with fork.

Just before serving, deep-fry crescents in hot oil until lightly browned and cooked through; drain on absorbent paper. Serve crescents hot with sauce.

Filling: Heat oil in pan, add garlic and onion, cook, stirring, until onion is soft. Add mince, cook, stirring, until well browned. Stir in parsley, curry powder, paste, vinegar and pepper. Cook, uncovered, for 10 minutes, stir in blended flour and water, stir over heat until mixture boils and thickens; cool.

Tomato Sauce: Heat oil in pan, add garlic and onion, cook, stirring, until onion is soft. Stir in undrained crushed tomatoes, paste and sugar, bring to boil, simmer, uncovered, for about 10 minutes or until thick. Blend or process sauce until smooth, strain.

Makes about 60.
■ Crescents and sauce can be prepared a day ahead.
■ Storage: Covered, in refrigerator.
■ Freeze: Uncooked crescents suitable.
■ Microwave: Not suitable.

LAMB STICKS WITH HERB YOGURT DIP

750g lean lamb, minced
1 onion, grated
1 clove garlic, crushed
1 teaspoon ground cinnamon
2 teaspoons paprika
2 teaspoons ground cumin
¼ teaspoon chilli powder
2 tablespoons chopped fresh mint
¼ cup chopped fresh parsley
1 tablespoon dry red wine

HERB YOGURT DIP
500g carton plain yogurt
2 cloves garlic, crushed
1 tablespoon chopped fresh parsley
2 tablespoons chopped fresh mint
1 tablespoon chopped fresh chives

Combine lamb, onion, garlic, spices, herbs and wine in bowl; mix well. Shape a level tablespoon of mixture around 1 end of skewers.

Just before serving, grill sticks until well browned all over and cooked through. Serve hot with dip.

Herb Yogurt Dip: Combine all ingredients in bowl; mix well.

Makes about 40.
■ Sticks and sauce can be prepared a day ahead.
■ Storage: Covered, in refrigerator.
■ Freeze: Uncooked sticks suitable. Sauce not suitable.
■ Microwave: Not suitable.

ABOVE LEFT: From front: Lamb Sticks with Herb Yogurt Dip, Curried Crescents with Tomato Sauce.
ABOVE RIGHT: Golden Fish Bites.
Above left: Plates from Made in Japan. Above right: Plates from Kenwick Galleries

GOLDEN FISH BITES

250g boneless white fish fillets
2 green shallots, chopped
2 teaspoons light soy sauce
1 egg white
1 teaspoon cornflour
15 slices fresh white bread
oil for deep-frying

SAUCE
2 teaspoons cornflour
2 tablespoons lemon juice
1 teaspoon light soy sauce
1 small chicken stock cube, crumbled
½ cup water
1 green shallot, chopped

Blend or process fish until finely minced. Transfer fish to bowl, stir in shallots, sauce, egg white and cornflour; mix well Remove crusts from bread, cut bread into 5mm cubes. Using damp hands, roll level teaspoons of fish mixture into balls, toss in bread cubes, press cubes on firmly; cover, refrigerate 30 minutes.

Just before serving, deep-fry bites in hot oil until lightly browned and cooked through. Serve hot with sauce.

Sauce: Blend cornflour with juice in pan, stir in remaining ingredients, stir over heat until sauce boils and thickens.

Makes about 40.
■ Bites can be prepared a day ahead.
■ Storage: Covered, in refrigerator.
■ Freeze: Suitable.
■ Microwave: Not suitable.

CHEESE AND VEGETABLE KEBABS IN CURRIED BATTER

300g broccoli, chopped
300g cauliflower, chopped
125g tasty cheese, cubed
plain flour
oil for deep-frying

BATTER
1½ cups self-raising flour
2 teaspoons curry powder
¼ teaspoon garam masala
1½ teaspoons sugar
2 eggs, separated
2½ cups milk

YOGURT DIP
200g carton plain yogurt
1 teaspoon chopped fresh chives
⅓ cup chopped walnuts or pecans

Boil, steam or microwave broccoli and cauliflower until just tender, rinse under cold water, drain on absorbent paper. Thread broccoli, cauliflower and cheese onto skewers, toss in flour, shake away excess flour.

Just before serving, dip kebabs in batter, deep-fry in hot oil until lightly browned, drain on absorbent paper. Serve kebabs hot with dip.

Batter: Sift dry ingredients into large bowl, gradually stir in egg yolks and milk, mix to a smooth batter.

Just before serving, whisk egg whites in small bowl until soft peaks form, fold gently into batter.

Yogurt Dip: Combine all ingredients in bowl, mix well.

Makes about 24.

■ Cheese and vegetables can be threaded onto skewers several hours ahead. Batter without egg whites can be prepared several hours ahead.
■ Storage: Both, covered, in refrigerator.
■ Freeze: Not suitable.
■ Microwave: Vegetables suitable.

ABOVE: Cheese and Vegetable Kebabs in Curried Batter.
RIGHT: Mushroom Palmiers.

Above: Plate from Opus. Right: Plate from Oceanfront Galleries

MUSHROOM PALMIERS

375g packet frozen puff pastry,
    thawed
1 egg, lightly beaten
FILLING
1 tablespoon oil
15g butter
2 cloves garlic, crushed
1 onion, finely chopped
250g mushrooms, finely chopped
1 tablespoon plain flour
2 tablespoons water
2 tablespoons chopped fresh chives

Roll pastry on lightly floured surface to 25cm x 35cm rectangle, cut in half lengthways to form 2 rectangles. Spread half the filling over 1 rectangle; repeat with remaining filling and rectangle.

Fold in long sides of each rectangle so they meet in the centre, brush along centre with some of the egg, fold in half, press lightly; cover, refrigerate 30 minutes. Cut rolls into 1cm slices, place with cut side up on lightly greased oven trays, bake in moderately hot oven for about 12 minutes or until well browned. Serve palmiers hot.

Filling: Heat oil and butter in pan, add garlic and onion, cook, stirring, until onion is soft. Stir in mushrooms, cook for about 5 minutes or until mushrooms are soft, stirring often. Add flour, stir over heat for 1 minute, gradually stir in water, stir over heat until mixture boils and thickens. Remove from heat; cool. Stir chives into mushroom mixture.

   Makes about 30.

- Palmiers can be made 2 days ahead.
- Storage: Covered, in refrigerator.
- Freeze: Not suitable.
- Microwave: Not suitable.

PRAWN AND VEGETABLE FRITTERS

200g cooked shelled small prawns
1 carrot
6 green shallots
2 eggs
1²⁄₃ cups iced water
2 cups plain flour
100g bean sprouts
oil for deep-frying
DIPPING SAUCE
2 tablespoons dark soy sauce
2 teaspoons fish sauce
2 tablespoons mirin
2 thin slices fresh ginger

Flatten prawns slightly. Cut carrot into very thin strips about 4cm long. Cut shallots into 4cm lengths.

Lightly whisk eggs in bowl with water. Add sifted flour all at once, stir until just combined; do not beat.

Place 2 prawns, some carrot, shallots and bean sprouts in a heap on a plate, spoon over enough batter to cover, turn heap over, spoon batter over to cover. Using metal spatula, slide heaps into hot oil, deep-fry until lightly browned; drain on absorbent paper. Serve hot with sauce.

Dipping Sauce: Combine sauces, mirin and ginger in bowl.

Makes about 30.

■ Fritters can be made 3 hours ahead; re-fry to serve.
■ Storage: Covered, in refrigerator.
■ Freeze: Not suitable.
■ Microwave: Not suitable.

CHICKEN LIVER MORSELS WITH BACON

250g chicken livers, trimmed
2 tablespoons dark soy sauce
2 tablespoons dry sherry
2 tablespoons lemon juice
1 clove garlic, crushed
1 teaspoon grated fresh ginger
1 tablespoon oil
10 bacon rashers
227g can sliced water chestnuts

Cut livers into 2cm pieces, combine in bowl with sauce, sherry, juice, garlic and ginger; cover, refrigerate 2 hours.

Heat oil in pan, add liver mixture, cook, stirring, for about 5 minutes or until livers are lightly browned all over and tender. Drain livers, discard liquid; cool.

Cut each bacon rasher into 3 pieces. Wrap a piece of liver and a slice of chestnut in a piece of bacon, secure with a toothpick. Repeat with remaining livers, chestnuts and bacon.

Just before serving, grill morsels until bacon is crisp and lightly browned.

Makes about 30.

■ Liver can be prepared a day ahead.
■ Storage: Covered, in refrigerator.
■ Freeze: Not suitable.
■ Microwave: Not suitable.

ROASTED RED PEPPER AND ONION TARTLETS

1 sheet ready rolled shortcrust pastry
1 small red pepper
100g baby onions, halved
1 clove garlic, halved
1 tablespoon olive oil
1 tablespoon sour cream
1 egg
1 teaspoon chopped fresh basil

Lightly grease 24 x 3½cm tart pans or mini muffin pans (1 tablespoon capacity).

Cut 24 x 5cm rounds from pastry, line prepared pans; prick all over with fork. Bake in moderately hot oven for about 12 minutes or until lightly browned; cool.

Cut pepper into quarters, remove seeds, place quarters with skin side up on oven tray. Place unpeeled onions and unpeeled garlic on oven tray with pepper. Brush vegetables with oil, bake in hot oven for about 15 minutes or until pepper skin blisters and browns; cool.

Remove skin from vegetables; chop onions finely. Blend or process pepper, garlic, sour cream, egg and basil until smooth and creamy.

Just before serving, divide onions between pastry cases, top with level teaspoons of pepper mixture. Bake in moderately hot oven for about 12 minutes or until set. Serve warm.

Makes 24.

■ Cases and filling can be prepared separately a day ahead.
■ Storage: Pastry cases in airtight container. Filling, covered, in refrigerator.
■ Freeze: Not suitable.
■ Microwave: Not suitable.

LEFT: Clockwise from front: Chicken Liver Morsels with Bacon, Prawn and Vegetable Fritters, Roasted Red Pepper and Onion Tartlets.

Plates from Made in Japan

KUMARA CUMIN PUFFS

½ cup water
40g butter
½ cup plain flour
¼ teaspoon turmeric
2 eggs
2 teaspoons chopped fresh chives
1 egg, lightly beaten, extra
FILLING
250g kumara, chopped
1 medium (100g) potato, chopped
1 medium onion, finely grated
½ teaspoon ground cumin
¼ cup sour cream

Combine water and butter in pan, bring to boil, stirring, until butter is melted. Add sifted flour and turmeric all at once, stir vigorously over heat until mixture leaves side of pan and forms a smooth ball.

Transfer mixture to small bowl of electric mixer (or into processor). Add eggs 1 at a time, beat on low speed until smooth after each addition, stir in chives.

Spoon mixture into piping bag fitted with 8mm plain tube, pipe small balls or drop ½ level teaspoons of mixture about 2cm apart onto lightly greased oven trays. Gently brush each ball lightly with extra egg. Bake in hot oven for 10 minutes, reduce heat to moderate, bake further 5 minutes or until puffs are lightly browned and crisp. Cool on wire rack.

Cut each puff in half. Spoon or pipe filling into each puff base, replace tops, place onto oven trays.

Just before serving, reheat in moderate oven for about 5 minutes.

Filling: Boil, steam or microwave kumara and potato until tender; drain. Mash well in bowl, stir in onion, cumin and sour cream, stir until well combined.

Makes about 70.
- Puffs and filling can be made separately a day ahead. Puffs can be filled an hour ahead.
- Storage: Unfilled puffs in airtight container. Filling, covered, in refrigerator.
- Freeze: Unfilled puffs suitable.
- Microwave: Filling suitable.

MINI BEEF MIGNONS

350g piece beef fillet
15 slices prosciutto
2 tablespoons oil

BEARNAISE SAUCE
⅓ cup white vinegar
6 black peppercorns
1 bay leaf
2 green shallots, chopped
2 tablespoons chopped fresh
   tarragon
2 egg yolks
250g butter, melted
2 teaspoons chopped fresh
   tarragon, extra

Cut beef into 2cm pieces. Cut prosciutto in halves lengthways. Wrap a piece of prosciutto around a piece of steak, secure with a toothpick. Repeat with remaining prosciutto and steak.

Just before serving, heat half the oil in pan, add half the steak, cook over high heat until browned all over and tender. Repeat with remaining oil and steak. Serve hot with sauce.

Bearnaise Sauce: Combine vinegar, peppercorns, bay leaf, shallots and tarragon in pan, bring to boil, simmer, uncovered, until reduced by half. Strain mixture, reserve liquid.

Blend or process egg yolks and reserved liquid until smooth. Gradually pour in hot bubbling butter while motor is operating, blend until thick and smooth. Stir in extra tarragon.

Makes about 30.
- Mignons can be prepared a day ahead; sauce made an hour ahead.
- Storage: Mignons, covered, in refrigerator. Sauce, covered, at room temperature.
- Freeze: Not suitable.
- Microwave: Not suitable.

MARINATED LAMB RIBLETS

2kg lamb riblets
½ cup ginger wine
½ cup dry white wine
1 cup oil
2 tablespoons plum sauce
3 cloves garlic, crushed
2 teaspoons sugar
2 tablespoons grated fresh ginger
2 teaspoons chopped fresh rosemary

Trim 3cm of meat from the bone at one end of each riblet. Combine riblets in bowl with remaining ingredients; cover, refrigerate overnight.

Just before serving, wrap ends of riblets in foil, grill until well browned and tender.
   Makes about 30.
- Riblets can be prepared 2 days ahead.
- Storage: Covered, in refrigerator.
- Freeze: Uncooked riblets suitable.
- Microwave: Not suitable.

LEFT: From front: Kumara Cumin Puffs, Mini Beef Mignons.
BELOW: Marinated Lamb Riblets.

Below: China from Villeroy and Boch; tiles from Country Floors

CRISP LITTLE POTATO ROSTI WITH LEMON CHIVE CREAM

30g butter
1 onion, chopped
3 medium (320g) old potatoes, coarsely grated
20g butter, extra
1 tablespoon oil
LEMON CHIVE CREAM
90g packaged cream cheese
2 tablespoons sour cream
1 teaspoon grated lemon rind
1 tablespoon lemon juice
1 tablespoon chopped fresh chives

Heat butter in pan, add onion, cook, stirring, until soft. Add potatoes, stir until potatoes are sticky; cool.

Shape level teaspoons of potato mixture into rounds with wet fingers; flatten slightly. Heat extra butter and oil in pan, add rosti, cook on each side for about 3 minutes or until well browned. Serve warm topped with lemon chive cream and extra chives, if desired.

Lemon Chive Cream: Beat cheese and sour cream in bowl with wooden spoon until smooth, beat in rind, juice and chives.
    Makes about 40.
■ Rosti can be made 3 hours ahead.
■ Storage: At room temperature.
■ Freeze: Not suitable.
■ Microwave: Not suitable.

CHICKEN AND PIMIENTO BASKETS

2 sheets fillo pastry
40g butter, melted
FILLING
200g can pimientos, drained, chopped
½ cup chopped cooked chicken
1 tablespoon cornflour
½ cup cream
1 teaspoon French mustard
1 tablespoon chopped fresh parsley

Cut each sheet of pastry into 8 strips lengthways. Cut each strip into 6 pieces; cover with plastic wrap. Brush 4 rectangles with butter, layer together at

angles, place in 1 hole of a mini muffin pan (1 tablespoon capacity). Repeat with remaining rectangles and butter. Bake in moderate oven for about 5 minutes or until lightly browned. Remove pastry baskets from pan, place onto oven tray.

Just before serving, spoon filling into pastry baskets, bake in moderate oven for about 5 minutes or until heated through.

Filling: Combine pimientos and chicken in pan, stir in blended cornflour and cream. Stir over heat until mixture boils and thickens, stir in mustard and parsley; cool to room temperature.

    Makes 24.
■ Baskets can be baked 2 days ahead. Filling can be prepared 3 hours ahead.
■ Storage: Unfilled baskets, in airtight container. Filling, covered, in refrigerator.
■ Freeze: Not suitable.
■ Microwave: Filling suitable.

SMOKED SALMON AND CAMEMBERT PUFFS

200g peppered camembert
2 sheets ready rolled puff pastry
100g smoked salmon, sliced
½ lime, thinly sliced
fresh dill sprigs

Remove rind from cheese, cut cheese into 5cm squares. Cut 5½cm rounds from pastry, place in ungreased 12-hole tart trays, top with cheese.

Just before serving, bake puffs in moderate oven for about 25 minutes or until browned. Remove puffs from trays, top with salmon, lime wedges and dill.
    Makes about 30.

■ Tart trays can be lined a day ahead.
■ Storage: Covered, in refrigerator.
■ Freeze: Not suitable.
■ Microwave: Not suitable.

LEFT: Crisp Little Potato Rosti with Lemon Chive Cream.
BELOW: From left: Chicken and Pimiento Baskets, Smoked Salmon and Camembert Puffs.

Left: Plate from Kenwick Galleries

CHICKEN AND CORN IN CREPE CUPS

½ cup plain flour
2 eggs, lightly beaten
2 teaspoons oil
½ cup milk
1 tablespoon chopped fresh chives
FILLING
30g butter
¼ teaspoon dry mustard
½ onion, finely chopped
50g mushrooms, finely chopped
1½ tablespoons plain flour
½ cup milk
1 chicken breast fillet, finely chopped
½ x 130g can creamed corn

Sift flour into bowl, gradually stir in combined eggs, oil and milk, beat to a smooth batter (or blend or process all ingredients until smooth); cover, stand 30 minutes.

Pour 2 to 3 tablespoons of batter into heated greased heavy-based crepe pan, cook until lightly browned underneath. Turn crepe, brown on other side. Repeat with remaining batter.

Cut 5½cm rounds from crepes.

Just before serving, line mini muffin pans (1 tablespoon capacity) with crepe rounds, bake in moderately hot oven for 10 minutes. Spoon filling into cases, bake further 5 minutes or until heated through. Sprinkle with chives.

Filling: Heat butter in pan, stir in mustard, onion and mushrooms, cook, stirring, until onion is soft. Stir in flour, cook 1 minute. Remove from heat, gradually stir in milk, chicken and corn, stir over heat until sauce boils and thickens. Simmer, covered, until chicken is tender; cool.

Makes about 55.
- ■ Cups and filling can be prepared separately 2 days ahead.
- ■ Storage: Covered, in refrigerator.
- ■ Freeze: Crepes suitable.
- ■ Microwave: Filling suitable.

BEEF EN CROUTE WITH GLAZED ONION

1 tablespoon oil
200g piece Scotch fillet steak
1 clove garlic, crushed
½ onion, sliced
1 tablespoon honey
5 thick slices white bread
60g butter, melted
1 tablespoon seeded mustard

Heat oil in pan, add steak, cook over high heat on each side until tender. Remove steak from pan, stand 5 minutes before slicing thinly. Add garlic and onion to same pan, cook, stirring, until onion is soft. Stir in honey, remove from heat.

Cut 4 x 4cm rounds from each slice of bread. Brush rounds on both sides with butter, place on oven tray. Bake in moderate oven for about 10 minutes or until lightly browned and crisp.

Just before serving, spread rounds with a little mustard, top with steak and a small amount of onion, place on oven tray. Bake in moderate oven for about 5 minutes or until heated through.

Makes 20.
- ■ Croutes can be prepared 2 days ahead. Steak and onion can be prepared 2 hours ahead.
- ■ Storage: Croutes in airtight container. Steak and onion, covered, in refrigerator.
- ■ Freeze: Croutes suitable.
- ■ Microwave: Not suitable.

COCONUT PRAWNS WITH MANGO SAUCE

500g large uncooked prawns, shelled
cornflour
1 egg white, lightly beaten
1 cup (70g) shredded coconut
oil for deep-frying

MANGO SAUCE
425g can mango slices, drained
2 tablespoons mayonnaise
2 tablespoons mango chutney

Toss prawns in cornflour, shake away excess cornflour. Dip prawns in egg white, then coconut.

Just before serving, deep-fry prawns in hot oil until lightly browned and tender. Serve hot with sauce.

Mango Sauce: Blend or process mango, mayonnaise and chutney until smooth.

Makes about 18.
- ■ Prawns and sauce can be prepared a day ahead.
- ■ Storage: Both, covered, in refrigerator.
- ■ Freeze: Not suitable.
- ■ Microwave: Not suitable.

LEFT: Clockwise from left: Coconut Prawns with Mango Sauce, Chicken and Corn in Crepe Cups, Beef en Croute with Glazed Onion.

Plates from Corso de Fiori

SCALLOP AND BACON BITES

¼ teaspoon ground nutmeg
¼ teaspoon garam masala
½ teaspoon five spice powder
¼ cup light soy sauce
1 tablespoon oil
¼ teaspoon sugar
500g scallops
10 bacon rashers

Combine spices, sauce, oil and sugar in bowl, stir in scallops; cover, refrigerate several hours.

Cut each bacon rasher crossways into 3 pieces, wrap scallops in bacon pieces, secure with toothpicks.

Just before serving, grill bites until bacon is lightly browned.

Makes about 30.

■ Bites can be prepared a day ahead.
■ Storage: Covered, in refrigerator.
■ Freeze: Not suitable.
■ Microwave: Not suitable.

GARLIC CHICKEN KEBABS

700g chicken breast fillets
½ cup light soy sauce
1 teaspoon grated lemon rind
¼ cup lemon juice
2 tablespoons sugar
2 tablespoons oil
CREAMY GARLIC SAUCE
½ cup cream
½ cup sour cream
2 cloves garlic, crushed

Cut chicken into 2cm pieces, combine in bowl with sauce, rind, juice, sugar and oil; cover, refrigerate 2 hours.

Thread chicken onto skewers.

Just before serving, grill kebabs until chicken is lightly browned and tender, serve hot with hot sauce.

Creamy Garlic Sauce: Combine all ingredients in pan, bring to boil, simmer, uncovered, for about 5 minutes or until slightly thickened.

Makes about 15.
■ Kebabs can be prepared a day ahead.
■ Storage: Covered, in refrigerator.
■ Freeze: Uncooked chicken suitable.
■ Microwave: Sauce suitable.

KUMARA AND SESAME FINGERS

You will need 750g kumara for this recipe.
3 eggs
¼ cup orange juice
¼ cup sour cream
2 teaspoons chopped fresh chives
¼ teaspoon ground cinnamon
¼ teaspoon ground cumin
2 cups cooked mashed kumara
3 teaspoons sesame seeds

Lightly grease 20cm x 30cm lamington pan, place strip of baking paper to cover base and extend over 2 opposite sides.

Whisk eggs until combined, whisk in juice, cream, chives, spices and kumara. Pour mixture into prepared pan, sprinkle evenly with seeds. Bake in moderate oven for about 20 minutes or until firm. Cut while hot.

Makes about 50.
■ Slice can be made a day ahead.
■ Storage: Covered, in refrigerator.
■ Freeze: Not suitable.
■ Microwave: Not suitable.

CRUNCHY POTATO SKINS WITH SOUR CREAM

4 large potatoes
2 tablespoons oil
1 teaspoon dry mustard
1 teaspoon seasoned pepper
300g carton sour cream

Scrub potatoes, bake in hot oven for about 50 minutes or until tender. Cut potatoes into eighths, scoop out flesh carefully, leaving skins intact (reserve flesh for another recipe).

Combine oil, mustard and pepper, brush over potato skins, place on oven tray with skin side up.

Just before serving, bake skins in hot oven for about 10 minutes or until crisp. Serve hot with sour cream. Serve sprinkled with coarse sea salt, if desired.

Makes 32.
■ Skins can be prepared for cooking a day ahead.
■ Storage: Covered, in refrigerator.
■ Freeze: Not suitable.
■ Microwave: Not suitable.

LEFT: Clockwise from front: Kumara and Sesame Fingers, Scallop and Bacon Bites, Garlic Chicken Kebabs.
ABOVE: Crunchy Potato Skins with Sour Cream.

Left: Plate from Kenwick Galleries

SPICED FISH NIBBLES

300g boneless white fish fillets, skinned
½ cup packaged breadcrumbs
1 egg
1 teaspoon grated fresh ginger
¼ teaspoon chilli powder
3 teaspoons ground coriander
oil for deep-frying

Blend or process fish, breadcrumbs, egg, ginger and spices until mixture forms a ball. Roll 2 level teaspoons of mixture into a ball; repeat with remaining mixture.

Just before serving, deep-fry nibbles in hot oil until lightly browned and cooked through. Serve hot drizzled with lemon juice, if desired.

Makes about 30.
■ Nibbles can be prepared a day ahead.
■ Storage: Covered, in refrigerator.
■ Freeze: Uncooked nibbles suitable.
■ Microwave: Not suitable.

CHICKEN AND RED PEPPER PASTIES

1 cup self-raising flour
3 cups plain flour
250g butter
2 egg yolks, lightly beaten
½ cup water, approximately
1 egg, lightly beaten
paprika

FILLING
20g butter
1 tablespoon oil
2 onions, chopped
450g chicken thigh fillets, chopped
3 teaspoons French mustard
½ red pepper, finely chopped

Sift flours into bowl, rub in butter. Stir in egg yolks with enough water to mix to a firm dough. Knead dough on floured surface until smooth; cover, refrigerate 30 minutes.

Cut pastry in half, roll each half on lightly floured surface until 2mm thick. Cut into 9cm rounds, top each round with 2 level teaspoons of filling. Lightly brush edges with water, fold in half, press edges together to seal. Place pasties, standing upright, onto lightly greased oven trays, brush with egg, sprinkle with paprika.

Just before serving, bake pasties in moderately hot oven for about 20 minutes or until well browned.

Filling: Heat butter and oil in pan, add onions, cook, stirring, until onions are soft. Add chicken, cook for about 5 minutes or until tender. Blend or process mixture until chicken is finely chopped, transfer mixture to bowl, stir in mustard and pepper.

Makes about 45.
■ Pasties can be prepared a day ahead.
■ Storage: Covered, in refrigerator.
■ Freeze: Uncooked pasties suitable.
■ Microwave: Not suitable.

MINI PIZZA SWIRLS

1 teaspoon sugar
1 sachet (7g) dry yeast
¼ cup warm water
1½ cups plain flour
1 teaspoon salt
1 tablespoon oil
½ cup warm water, extra, approximately
TOMATO SAUCE
1 teaspoon oil
1 clove garlic, crushed
½ cup tomato paste
2 tablespoons tomato sauce
1 teaspoon dried oregano leaves
TOPPING
1 small onion, finely chopped
½ small green pepper, finely chopped
2 hard-boiled eggs, chopped
⅓ cup grated mozzarella cheese

Combine sugar, yeast and water in bowl; cover, stand in warm place for about 10 minutes or until foamy.

Sift flour and salt into bowl, stir in yeast mixture, oil, and enough extra water to mix to a soft dough. Knead dough on lightly floured surface for 10 minutes. Place dough in lightly oiled bowl; cover, stand in warm place for about 45 minutes or until doubled in size.

Knead dough on lightly floured surface until smooth. Roll half the dough to a 20cm x 45cm rectangle, spread with half the tomato sauce, sprinkle with half the topping. Roll up tightly from long side, cut into 1cm slices, place slices cut side up on greased oven trays. Repeat with remaining dough, tomato sauce and topping. Bake in moderate oven for about 15 minutes or until well browned. Serve swirls hot.

Tomato Sauce: Heat oil in pan, add garlic, cook 1 minute, stir in paste, sauce and oregano; cool.

Topping: Combine all ingredients in bowl.
Makes about 60.
■ Swirls can be made 3 hours ahead.
■ Storage: At room temperature.
■ Freeze: Cooked swirls suitable.
■ Microwave: Tomato sauce suitable.

RIGHT: From left: Spiced Fish Nibbles, Chicken and Red Pepper Pasties, Mini Pizza Swirls.

HOT EGG DIP WITH SALAMI STICKS

250g packet cream cheese
¼ cup sour cream
¼ cup mayonnaise
1 tablespoon chopped fresh chives
1 teaspoon seeded mustard
6 hard-boiled eggs, chopped

SALAMI STICKS
70cm French bread stick
180g butter
100g salami, chopped
1 tablespoon chopped fresh chives
1½ cups (185g) grated tasty cheese

Beat cream cheese in bowl until smooth, beat in sour cream, mayonnaise, chives and mustard, stir in eggs.

Just before serving, place egg mixture in pan, stir over low heat until warm; do not boil. Serve with hot salami sticks.
Salami Sticks: Cut bread stick in half crossways, split in halves lengthways. Beat butter in bowl until smooth, stir in salami and chives. Spread mixture evenly over bread, sprinkle with cheese, press cheese on firmly.
Just before serving, grill bread until cheese is melted. Cut bread into chunks.
Makes about 2 cups dip.
■ Dip and salami sticks can be prepared a day ahead.
■ Storage: Both, covered, in refrigerator.
■ Freeze: Salami sticks suitable.
■ Microwave: Not suitable.

SWEET POTATO SCONES WITH CREAMY HERB CHEESE

1 medium (375g) sweet potato
2 cups self-raising flour
2 teaspoons sugar
15g butter
1 cup milk, approximately

CREAMY HERB CHEESE
150g packaged cream cheese
2 tablespoons chopped fresh parsley
1 tablespoon chopped fresh chives

Lightly grease 23cm square slab pan. Place potato on oven tray, pierce with fork, bake in moderate oven for about 45 minutes or until tender; cool to room temperature. Peel and mash potato (you will need 1 cup of mashed potato).

Sift flour and sugar into bowl; rub in butter. Stir in potato and enough milk to mix to a soft dough. Turn dough onto lightly floured surface, knead gently until smooth. Press dough evenly on lightly floured surface until 1½cm thick; cut into 4cm rounds. Place scones in prepared pan; brush tops with a little extra milk.
Just before serving, bake scones in very hot oven for about 15 minutes or until tops are browned. Split scones in half, sandwich with herb cheese.
Creamy Herb Cheese: Beat cheese in small bowl with electric mixer until light and fluffy, stir in herbs.
Makes about 36.
■ Scones and herb cheese can be made 3 hours ahead.
■ Storage: Scones, covered, at room temperature. Herb cheese, covered, in refrigerator.
■ Freeze: Scones suitable.
■ Microwave: Not suitable.

CHICKEN AND SHALLOT SPRING ROLLS

200g chicken thigh fillets
5 green shallots
1 tablespoon grated fresh ginger
¼ cup dry sherry
⅓ cup light soy sauce
1½ tablespoons brown sugar
30 egg pastry sheets
oil for deep-frying

SAUCE
2 green shallots, finely sliced

Cut chicken into 1cm strips. Cut shallots into 4cm lengths, then halve lengthways. Combine chicken, shallots, ginger, sherry, sauce and sugar in bowl; cover, refrigerate 30 minutes.

Drain chicken and shallots; reserve marinade for sauce.

Lightly brush an edge of a pastry sheet with water. Place a piece of chicken and a few strips of shallot at opposite end, fold in sides, then roll up, pressing moistened end to seal. Repeat with remaining pastry, chicken and shallots.
Just before serving, deep-fry rolls in hot oil until well browned; drain on absorbent paper. Serve warm with sauce.

Sauce: Heat reserved marinade in pan, bring to boil, stir in shallots.

Makes 30.

■ Rolls can be made a day ahead.

■ Storage: Spring rolls and sauce, covered, in refrigerator.

■ Freeze: Uncooked spring rolls suitable.

■ Microwave: Sauce suitable.

LEFT: Hot Egg Dip with Salami Sticks.
ABOVE: From back: Sweet Potato Scones with Creamy Herb Cheese, Chicken and Shallot Spring Rolls.

Left: Serving ware from Villeroy and Boch

SPICY BEEF PUFFS WITH TOMATO SAUCE

250g minced beef
3 green shallots, finely chopped
2 tablespoons chopped fresh parsley
1/4 teaspoon garam masala
1/4 teaspoon five spice powder
1/4 teaspoon dry mustard
1 tablespoon tomato paste
1/2 cup grated tasty cheese
3 sheets ready rolled
   shortcrust pastry
oil for deep-frying

TOMATO SAUCE
300g can Tomato Supreme
1/4 teaspoon seasoned pepper
1 teaspoon Worcestershire sauce
1/2 teaspoon dry mustard
1 tablespoon chopped fresh chives

Cook mince in pan over high heat, stirring, until meat is browned and cooked. Stir in shallots, parsley, spices and paste, stir over heat until all liquid has evaporated. Remove from heat, stir in cheese.

Cut pastry into 5½cm rounds, top each round with 1 level teaspoon of mixture, lightly brush edges with water, fold in half, press edges together.

Just before serving, deep-fry puffs in hot oil until well browned; drain on absorbent paper. Serve hot with sauce.

Tomato Sauce: Combine Tomato Supreme, pepper, sauce, mustard and chives in pan, bring to boil.

Makes about 40.

■ Both can be prepared a day ahead.
■ Storage: Both, covered, in refrigerator.
■ Freeze: Uncooked puffs suitable.
■ Microwave: Sauce suitable.

CHEESY TOMATO BASIL MUSSELS

35 (1½kg) small mussels
1/2 cup dry white wine
40g butter
1 onion, finely chopped
2 cloves garlic, crushed
410g can tomatoes
2 tablespoons chopped fresh basil
60g gruyere cheese, grated

Scrub mussels, remove beards. Heat wine in large pan, add mussels, cook, covered, over high heat for about 5 minutes or until mussels open. Drain; discard liquid. Place each mussel in half a shell, place on oven tray.

Heat butter in pan, add onion and garlic, cook, stirring, until onion is soft. Stir in undrained crushed tomatoes, bring to boil, simmer, uncovered, for about 10 minutes or until thickened; stir in basil. Spoon mixture over mussels, sprinkle with cheese.

Just before serving, grill mussels until cheese is lightly browned.

Makes 35.

■ Can be prepared 3 hours ahead.
■ Storage: Covered, in refrigerator.
■ Freeze: Not suitable.
■ Microwave: Not suitable.

SMOKED TURKEY PUMPERNICKEL CANAPES

120g smoked turkey, finely chopped
1½ tablespoons sour cream
2 teaspoons horseradish cream
1 teaspoon chopped fresh chives
250g packet sliced pumpernickel
   rounds
100g Swiss cheese, thinly sliced

Combine turkey, sour cream, horseradish cream and chives in bowl. Place 1 level teaspoon of mixture onto each pumpernickel round, place rounds on baking paper-lined oven trays. Cut cheese into pieces large enough to cover rounds, place on top of turkey mixture.

Just before serving, bake canapes in hot oven until cheese is bubbling.

Makes about 24.

■ Canapes can be prepared several hours ahead.
■ Storage: Covered, in refrigerator.
■ Freeze: Not suitable.
■ Microwave: Not suitable.

RIGHT: Clockwise from back: Spicy Beef Puffs with Tomato Sauce, Cheesy Tomato Basil Mussels, Smoked Turkey Pumpernickel Canapes.

Platters from Made in Japan

SPINACH AND CHICKEN PINWHEELS

½ bunch (20 leaves) English spinach
2 tablespoons oil

CREPES
¾ cup plain flour
2 eggs, lightly beaten
¾ cup milk
2 teaspoons oil

FILLING
20g butter
2 green shallots, chopped
2 teaspoons canned drained green
    peppercorns, crushed
300g minced chicken
1 egg white, lightly beaten
½ cup stale breadcrumbs

Boil, steam or microwave spinach until tender, drain well; cool.

Place 2 crepes end to end, slightly over-lapping. Repeat with remaining crepes. Divide filling between crepes, spread filling evenly, cover filling with spinach leaves. Roll crepes up firmly from narrow ends like a Swiss roll; cover, refrigerate 30 minutes.

Just before serving, cut ends from rolls; discard ends. Cut each roll into 1cm slices, place a toothpick through centre of each slice.

Heat half the oil in pan, cook half the pinwheels until lightly browned on both sides and filling is cooked through, drain on absorbent paper. Repeat with remaining oil and pinwheels.

Crepes: Sift flour into bowl, gradually stir in combined eggs, milk and oil, mix to a smooth batter (or blend or process until smooth); cover, stand 30 minutes.

Pour 2 to 3 tablespoons of batter into heated greased heavy-based crepe pan; cook until lightly browned underneath. Turn crepe, brown on other side. Repeat with remaining batter. You will need 10 crepes for this recipe.

Filling: Heat butter in pan, stir in shallots and peppercorns, cook, stirring, until shallots are soft; cool. Combine chicken, egg white, crumbs and shallot mixture in bowl.

Makes about 50.

■ Rolls can be prepared 2 days ahead.
■ Storage: Covered, in refrigerator.
■ Freeze: Uncooked rolls suitable.
■ Microwave: Filling suitable.

NUTTY BEEF SATAYS

750g piece rump steak
½ cup crunchy peanut butter
1 small chicken stock cube, crumbled
1 cup water
2 tablespoons dry sherry
2 tablespoons honey
1 tablespoon dark soy sauce
1 tablespoon lime juice
2 teaspoons curry powder
1 teaspoon grated fresh ginger
1 teaspoon ground cumin
1 teaspoon ground coriander

Cut steak into 2cm cubes. Thread cubes onto 20 small skewers, place in single layer in shallow dish.

Combine remaining ingredients in bowl, pour over satay sticks; cover, refrigerate several hours or overnight.

Just before serving, drain satay sticks, reserve marinade. Bring marinade to boil in pan, boil, uncovered, for about 10 minutes, stirring frequently, or until thickened. Grill satay sticks until beef is tender. Serve with sauce.

Makes 20.

■ Sticks can be prepared 2 days ahead.
■ Storage: Covered, in refrigerator.
■ Freeze: Uncooked sticks suitable.
■ Microwave: Not suitable.

LEFT: From left: Nutty Beef Satays, Spinach and Chicken Pinwheels.

Bowl from Oceanfront Galleries

CHEESY MINI BURGERS

6 slices bread
60g butter, melted
1 tablespoon tomato paste
⅓ cup grated tasty cheese
MEAT PATTIES
250g minced beef
1 small onion, finely chopped
½ teaspoon French mustard
½ teaspoon tomato sauce
½ teaspoon Worcestershire sauce
1 tablespoon oil

Cut 4 x 4½cm rounds from each slice of bread. Brush rounds with butter, place on oven trays, bake in moderate oven for about 15 minutes or until lightly browned and crisp. Spread each round with tomato paste, top with a meat pattie and cheese.
Just before serving, grill burgers until cheese is melted.
Meat Patties: Combine mince, onion, mustard and sauces in bowl. Shape 2 level teaspoons of mixture into a ball, flatten to a 4cm pattie. Repeat with remaining mixture. Heat oil in pan, add patties, cook until well browned; drain on absorbent paper.

  Makes about 24.

■ Patties and bread rounds can be prepared a day ahead.
■ Storage: Patties, covered, in refrigerator.
■ Freeze: Uncooked patties suitable.
■ Microwave: Not suitable.

MUSHROOM CREAM PASTRIES

1 sheet ready rolled puff pastry
⅓ cup sour cream
¼ cup grated gruyere cheese
1 teaspoon seeded mustard
125g baby mushrooms, sliced
20g butter, melted
¼ cup grated gruyere cheese, extra

Spread pastry with combined sour cream, cheese and mustard. Cut pastry in halves, arrange mushrooms down centre of each half. Fold in long sides over mushrooms. Brush pastry with butter, cut into 2cm slices. Place slices on greased oven trays, sprinkle with extra cheese.
Just before serving, bake pastries in moderately hot oven for about 15 minutes or until lightly browned. Serve hot.

  Makes about 25.

■ Can be prepared 3 hours ahead.
■ Storage: Covered, in refrigerator.
■ Freeze: Not suitable.
■ Microwave: Not suitable.

STEAMED CHILLI PRAWNS

1 large (200g) carrot
45 (1kg) medium uncooked prawns, shelled
1 tablespoon honey
2 small fresh red chillies, chopped
¼ cup oil

Peel carrot into thin strips using vegetable peeler. Wrap a strip of carrot around each prawn, secure with toothpicks. Combine honey, chillies and oil in bowl, add prawns, mix well; cover, refrigerate 1 hour.
Just before serving, place prawns in steamer in single layer; cover, steam until prawns are tender.

  Makes 45.

■ Prawns can be prepared a day ahead.
■ Storage: Covered, in refrigerator.
■ Freeze: Not suitable.
■ Microwave: Suitable.

ABOVE: Cheesy Mini Burgers.
RIGHT: From top: Mushroom Cream Pastries, Steamed Chilli Prawns.

Above: Plate from Clay Things. Right: Bowl from Kenwick Galleries

FRESH ASPARAGUS AND SALMON PASTRIES

375g packet frozen puff pastry, thawed
60g butter, melted
2 tablespoons oil
8 medium spears fresh asparagus, chopped
1 clove garlic, crushed
1 teaspoon grated fresh ginger
3 green shallots, chopped
1 tablespoon dry sherry
2 teaspoons light soy sauce
1 tablespoon oyster sauce
½ cup water
1 small chicken stock cube, crumbled
2 teaspoons cornflour
2 teaspoons water, extra
210g can salmon, drained, flaked

Roll pastry on lightly floured surface until 4mm thick. Cut 4cm squares from pastry. Using 3cm square cutter, cut three-quarters through squares to make a border around edges. Place squares on oven tray, brush tops with butter, bake in moderately hot oven for about 12 minutes or until lightly browned. Remove and discard centres of squares.

Heat oil in pan, add asparagus, garlic and ginger, cook, stirring, for 5 minutes. Stir in shallots, sherry and sauces, then water and stock cube, bring to boil, simmer, uncovered, for 3 minutes. Stir in blended cornflour and extra water, stir until mixture boils and thickens. Stir in salmon; cool to room temperature.

Just before serving, spoon salmon mixture into pastry cases, place on oven trays, reheat in moderate oven for about 10 minutes.

Makes about 35.

- Pastry cases and filling can be made separately a day ahead.
- Storage: Pastry cases in airtight container. Filling, covered, in refrigerator.
- Freeze: Pastry cases suitable.
- Microwave: Not suitable.

LENTIL PIKELETS WITH LEEK AND MUSHROOM TOPPING

⅓ cup brown lentils
1 cup wholemeal self-raising flour
1 egg
¾ cup milk
2 tablespoons olive oil
½ teaspoon ground caraway
LEEK AND MUSHROOM TOPPING
60g butter
1 small leek, sliced
2 cloves garlic, crushed
250g baby mushrooms, sliced
320g jar sweet red peppers, drained, chopped
2 tablespoons chopped fresh tarragon

Add lentils to pan of boiling water, boil, uncovered, for about 15 minutes or until just tender; drain.

Blend or process flour, egg, milk, oil and caraway until smooth, stir in lentils. Drop level teaspoons of batter into heated non-stick pan, cook until bubbles appear; turn pikelets, brown other side.

Just before serving, top warm pikelets with hot topping.

Leek and Mushroom Topping: Heat butter in pan, add leek, cook over low heat for about 10 minutes. Add garlic and mushrooms, cook, stirring, until mushrooms are soft. Stir in peppers and tarragon; mix well.

Makes about 80.

- Pikelets can be made 3 hours ahead, reheat in oven. Topping can be made 1 hour ahead, reheat before serving.
- Storage: Pikelets, in airtight container. Topping, at room temperature.
- Freeze: Cooked pikelets suitable.
- Microwave: Topping suitable.

RIGHT: From left: Lentil Pikelets with Leek and Mushroom Topping, Fresh Asparagus and Salmon Pastries.

China from Villeroy & Boch

BACON AND EGG RAVIOLI WITH BASIL SAUCE

1⅓ cups plain flour
2 eggs, lightly beaten
2 tablespoons water, approximately
1 egg, lightly beaten, extra
oil for deep-frying

FILLING
1 teaspoon oil
1 small onion, finely chopped
1 bacon rasher, finely chopped
1 hard-boiled egg, finely chopped
1 teaspoon chopped fresh parsley

SAUCE
3 teaspoons butter
3 teaspoons plain flour
1¼ cups milk
1 tablespoon cream
2 teaspoons chopped fresh basil

Sift flour into bowl, stir in eggs with enough water to mix to a firm dough. Knead dough on lightly floured surface until smooth; cover, refrigerate 30 minutes. Roll dough on lightly floured surface until 3mm thick (or follow pasta machine instructions).

Cut 7½cm rounds from dough, cut rounds in half. Lightly brush semi-circles with extra egg, top each semi-circle with ½ level teaspoon of filling, fold in half, press edges together with a fork.

Add ravioli to large pan of boiling water, boil, uncovered, for 5 minutes, drain; pat dry with absorbent paper.

Just before serving, deep-fry ravioli in hot oil until lightly browned; drain on absorbent paper. Serve ravioli hot with warm sauce.

Filling: Heat oil in pan, add onion and bacon, cook, stirring, until onion is soft;

drain on absorbent paper. Combine onion mixture, egg and parsley in bowl; cool.
Sauce: Heat butter in pan, add flour, cook, stirring, until bubbling. Remove from heat, stir in milk and cream, stir over heat until sauce boils and thickens; stir in basil.

Makes about 40.

- Ravioli can be prepared a day ahead; sauce several hours ahead.
- Storage: Both, covered, in refrigerator.
- Freeze: Ravioli suitable before or after it has been boiled.
- Microwave: Sauce suitable.

MARINATED BEEF FRITTERS

2 (400g) Scotch fillet steaks
1 tablespoon oyster sauce
2 tablespoons light soy sauce
1 tablespoon dry sherry
1 small fresh red chilli, chopped
½ cup self-raising flour
1 teaspoon paprika
½ cup water
oil for deep-frying
¼ teaspoon cornflour

Trim fat from steaks, cut steaks into 2cm cubes, combine with sauces, sherry and chilli in bowl; cover, refrigerate several hours or overnight.

Sift flour and paprika into bowl, gradually stir in water, mix to a smooth batter (or blend or process all ingredients).

Just before serving, drain steak; reserve marinade. Dip pieces of steak into batter, deep-fry in hot oil until lightly browned and tender; drain on absorbent paper. Blend reserved marinade and cornflour in pan, stir over heat until sauce boils and thickens. Serve fritters hot with hot sauce.

Makes about 25.

■ Steak can be prepared a day ahead. Batter can be prepared 1 hour ahead.
■ Storage: Both, covered, in refrigerator.
■ Freeze: Uncooked steak suitable.
■ Microwave: Sauce suitable.

BEEF AND HORSERADISH BONBONS

4 slices (125g) sliced roast beef
4 sheets fillo pastry
60g butter, melted
2 teaspoons chopped fresh parsley
2 teaspoons chopped fresh chives
1 tablespoon horseradish cream

Cut each beef slice into 8 strips. Brush a sheet of pastry with combined butter, parsley, chives and horseradish, top with another pastry sheet, brush with more butter mixture. Cut pastry into quarters, cut each quarter into quarters again.

Top each quarter with a strip of beef, roll up from narrow sides, pinch ends to form bonbon shapes. Repeat with remaining pastry, butter mixture and beef. Place bonbons on lightly greased oven trays.

Just before serving, bake bonbons in hot oven for about 8 minutes or until lightly browned and crisp.

Makes 32.

■ Bonbons can be prepared a day ahead.
■ Storage: Covered, in refrigerator.
■ Freeze: Uncooked bonbons suitable.
■ Microwave: Not suitable.

ABOVE LEFT: From back: Marinated Beef Fritters, Bacon and Egg Ravioli with Basil Sauce.
ABOVE RIGHT: From top: Creamy Egg and Chive Croquettes, Beef and Horseradish Bonbons.

Above right: China from Limoges

CREAMY EGG AND CHIVE CROQUETTES

40g butter
1 onion, finely chopped
⅓ cup plain flour
1 cup milk
2 tablespoons chopped fresh chives
5 hard-boiled eggs, chopped
2 tablespoons sour cream
2 teaspoons chopped fresh thyme
5 cups (500g) stale breadcrumbs
3 eggs, lightly beaten
2 tablespoons milk, extra
oil for deep-frying

Heat butter in pan, add onion, cook, stirring, until soft. Stir in flour, cook until bubbling. Remove from heat, gradually stir in milk. Stir over heat until mixture boils and thickens; cool. Stir in chives, eggs, sour cream and thyme.

Shape level tablespoons of mixture into croquettes, roll in breadcrumbs, dip in combined eggs and extra milk, then breadcrumbs again.

Just before serving, deep-fry croquettes in hot oil until golden brown.

Makes about 30.

■ Can be prepared a day ahead.
■ Storage: Covered, in refrigerator.
■ Freeze: Cooked croquettes suitable.
■ Microwave: Not suitable.

CHICKEN GINGER ROLLS

1½ cups plain flour
1 egg yolk
60g lard
⅓ cup water
1 egg, lightly beaten
2 teaspoons rock salt
FILLING
250g minced chicken
1 egg white
1 small onion, grated
2 tablespoons chopped glace ginger
½ cup stale breadcrumbs
2 tablespoons chopped fresh chives

Sift flour into bowl, add yolk, cover with some of the flour. Place lard and water into pan, stir over low heat until lard is melted, bring to boil. Pour boiling liquid into flour all at once, mix to a firm dough. Turn dough onto lightly floured surface; knead until smooth; cover, stand 10 minutes.

Divide dough into 2 portions, roll each portion on lightly floured surface into 12cm x 30cm rectangle. Place half the filling down centre of 1 rectangle, brush edges with some of the egg. Fold edges over to cover filling. Repeat with remaining rectangle, filling and more egg.

Place rolls seam side down on lightly greased oven tray. Brush rolls with egg, sprinkle lightly with salt. Bake in moderately hot oven for about 25 minutes or until well browned. Stand rolls 5 minutes before slicing. Serve hot.
Filling: Combine all ingredients in bowl.
Makes about 60.
■ Rolls can be made a day ahead.
■ Storage: Covered, in refrigerator.
■ Freeze: Cooked rolls suitable.
■ Microwave: Not suitable.

CHEESY PASTRAMI PUFFS

40g butter
½ cup water
½ cup plain flour
2 eggs, lightly beaten
¼ cup grated fresh parmesan cheese
FILLING
60g butter
2 green shallots, chopped
1 red pepper, finely chopped
¼ cup plain flour
1 cup milk
5 slices (60g) pastrami, finely chopped
½ teaspoon paprika

Combine butter and water in pan, bring to boil, stirring, until butter is melted. Stir in sifted flour all at once, stir vigorously over heat until mixture leaves side of pan and forms a smooth ball. Transfer mixture to small bowl of electric mixer (or food

processor). Add eggs gradually, beating well between each addition; beat in cheese. Spoon level teaspoons of mixture onto greased oven trays, bake in moderately hot oven for 12 minutes, reduce heat to moderate, bake further 5 minutes or until lightly browned and crisp. Cut puffs in half, turn oven off; leave puffs to dry out in oven.

Just before serving, join puffs with filling, place on oven tray, reheat in moderate oven for about 5 minutes.

Filling: Heat butter in pan, add shallots and pepper, cook, stirring, until pepper is soft. Stir in flour, stir until bubbling. Remove from heat, gradually stir in milk, then pastrami and paprika. Stir over heat until mixture boils and thickens.

Makes about 65.
- Puffs and filling can be made separately a day ahead.
- Storage: Puffs, in airtight container. Filling, covered, in refrigerator.
- Freeze: Unfilled puffs suitable.
- Microwave: Filling suitable.

CRUMBED CHEESE CUBES

Leyden is a firm, caraway-flavoured cheese with a texture similar to cheddar.
150g Leyden cheese
plain flour
1 egg, lightly beaten
2 tablespoons milk
¾ cup crushed nuts
¼ cup packaged breadcrumbs
oil for deep-frying

Cut cheese into 1cm cubes, toss in flour, shake away excess flour. Dip cubes in combined egg and milk, then combined nuts and breadcrumbs. Repeat with egg mixture then nut mixture; cover, refrigerate 30 minutes.

Just before serving, deep-fry cubes in hot oil until well browned, drain on absorbent paper. Serve hot.

Makes about 35.
- Cubes can be prepared a day ahead.
- Storage: Covered, in refrigerator.
- Freeze: Not suitable.
- Microwave: Not suitable.

QUAIL SCOTCH EGGS

12 quail eggs
275g minced chicken
1 tablespoon chopped fresh parsley
1 tablespoon chopped fresh chives
1 teaspoon dry mustard
plain flour
1 egg, lightly beaten
packaged breadcrumbs
oil for deep-frying

Place eggs in pan, barely cover with cold water, bring to boil, stirring gently to centre yolks. Simmer for 4 minutes, drain, place eggs in cold water, crack shells gently; cool to room temperature.

Combine chicken, herbs and mustard in bowl. Divide mixture into 12 portions.

Drain eggs, discard shells. Toss eggs in flour, shake away excess flour. Shape each portion of chicken mixture around each egg, using lightly floured hands. Dip each egg in beaten egg, then into breadcrumbs.

Just before serving, deep-fry eggs in hot oil until well browned; drain on absorbent paper. Cut eggs in halves.

Makes 24.
- Eggs can be prepared a day ahead.
- Storage: Covered, in refrigerator.
- Freeze: Not suitable.
- Microwave: Not suitable.

ABOVE LEFT: From back: Chicken Ginger Rolls, Cheesy Pastrami Puffs, Crumbed Cheese Cubes.
ABOVE: Quail Scotch Eggs.

Above left: Plate and tray from Made in Japan.
Above: Plate from Clay Things

Wrap steak in plastic wrap, freeze for about 20 minutes or until partially frozen. Remove plastic, cut steak into thin slices. Combine steak, sauce and mustard in bowl; cover, refrigerate 30 minutes.

Cut asparagus and pepper into 5cm strips. Boil, steam or microwave asparagus and pepper until just tender; drain. Wrap a piece of steak around a piece each of asparagus and pepper, secure with toothpick. Repeat with remaining steak, asparagus and pepper.

Just before serving, heat oil in pan, add rolls, cook until well browned all over.

Makes about 48.

- Rolls can be prepared a day ahead.
- Storage: Covered, in refrigerator.
- Freeze: Uncooked rolls suitable.
- Microwave: Not suitable.

CRUMBED SQUID WITH COCONUT CURRY SAUCE

200g packet cheese-flavoured corn chips
200g small squid hoods, thinly sliced
⅓ cup cornflour
1 egg, lightly beaten
1 tablespoon milk
oil for deep-frying

COCONUT CURRY SAUCE
1 teaspoon oil
1 clove garlic, crushed
2 teaspoons curry powder
½ teaspoon turmeric
2 teaspoons cornflour
1 cup coconut cream
½ teaspoon sugar

Blend or process corn chips until coarsely crushed. Toss squid in cornflour, shake away excess cornflour. Dip squid in combined egg and milk, then corn chips, pressing corn chips on firmly; cover, refrigerate 1 hour.

Just before serving, deep-fry squid in hot oil for about 30 seconds or until lightly browned. Drain on absorbent paper, serve hot with hot sauce.

Coconut Curry Sauce: Heat oil in pan, add garlic, curry powder and turmeric, cook, stirring, for 2 minutes; remove from heat. Blend cornflour with 1 tablespoon of the coconut cream, stir into curry mixture with sugar. Gradually stir in remaining cream, stir until mixture boils and thickens; simmer 1 minute.

Makes about 50.

- Squid can be prepared a day ahead. Sauce can be made 1 hour ahead.
- Storage: Squid, covered, in refrigerator. Sauce, covered, at room temperature.
- Freeze: Uncooked squid suitable.
- Microwave: Not suitable.

BAKED LAMB CUTLETS IN HONEY SESAME MARINADE

12 lamb cutlets

HONEY SESAME MARINADE
¼ cup light soy sauce
1 clove garlic, crushed
1 tablespoon dry sherry
2 tablespoons honey
¼ teaspoon five spice powder
1 teaspoon sesame oil
1 teaspoon sesame seeds

Scrape cutlets down the bone to meaty section, trim away excess fat. Place cutlets in shallow dish, add marinade, turn to coat completely; cover, refrigerate several hours or overnight.

Just before serving, place cutlets on wire rack over baking dish, bake in moderate oven for about 35 minutes or until cutlets are tender. Brush with marinade during cooking.

Honey Sesame Marinade: Combine all ingredients in bowl.

Makes 12.

- Cutlets can be prepared 2 days ahead.
- Storage: Covered, in refrigerator.
- Freeze: Uncooked cutlets suitable.
- Microwave: Not suitable.

BEEF, ASPARAGUS AND PEPPER ROLLS

400g piece rump steak
3 teaspoons Worcestershire sauce
2 teaspoons seeded mustard
1 medium bunch (12 spears) fresh asparagus
1 red pepper
2 tablespoons oil

ABOVE LEFT: Baked Lamb Cutlets in Honey Sesame Marinade.
RIGHT: From top: Crumbed Squid with Coconut Curry Sauce, Beef, Asparagus and Pepper Rolls.

CRISPY CRAB TRIANGLES

60g butter
3 green shallots, chopped
¼ cup plain flour
1 cup milk
1 tablespoon lime juice
1 tablespoon chopped fresh parsley
2 x 170g cans crab meat, drained
16 sheets fillo pastry
180g butter, melted, extra

Heat butter in pan, add shallots, cook, stirring, until soft. Stir in flour, stir until bubbling. Remove from heat, gradually stir in milk, stir over heat until mixture boils and thickens. Stir in juice, parsley and crab; cool to room temperature.

Brush 2 sheets of pastry with some of the extra butter, layer together, cut crossways into 7cm strips. Place a level teaspoon of crab mixture at 1 end of each strip. Fold ends over to form triangles, continue folding to end of strips, brush with butter. Place triangles on lightly greased oven tray. Repeat with remaining pastry, butter and filling.

Just before serving, bake triangles in moderate oven for about 15 minutes or until lightly browned.

Makes about 60.
- Triangles can be prepared a day ahead.
- Storage: Covered, in refrigerator.
- Freeze: Uncooked triangles suitable.
- Microwave: Not suitable.

CHICKEN COCONUT BITES

3 cups (150g) flaked coconut
2 chicken breast fillets
plain flour
1 egg, lightly beaten
2 tablespoons milk
oil for deep-frying
1 teaspoon celery salt
½ teaspoon garlic powder
½ teaspoon ground cumin

Blend or process coconut until roughly chopped. Cut chicken into 2cm pieces. Toss chicken in flour, shake away excess flour. Dip chicken into combined egg and milk, then into coconut. Press coconut firmly onto chicken; cover, refrigerate 15 minutes.

Just before serving, deep-fry chicken in hot oil until golden brown and tender. Drain on absorbent paper, sprinkle with combined salt, garlic powder and cumin.

Makes about 40.
- Bites can be prepared a day ahead.
- Storage: Covered, in refrigerator.
- Freeze: Uncooked bites suitable.
- Microwave: Not suitable.

CREAMY SMOKED SALMON TARTLETS

3 sheets ready rolled puff pastry
100g smoked salmon, finely chopped
2 gherkins, finely chopped
2 green shallots, chopped
½ cup sour cream
1 tablespoon milk
2 eggs, lightly beaten
1 teaspoon chopped fresh dill
¼ teaspoon paprika

Cut pastry into 6½cm rounds, place rounds into lightly greased 12-hole tart trays. Sprinkle salmon, gherkins and shallots into pastry shells, pour in combined cream, milk, eggs, dill and paprika. Bake in moderate oven for about 30 minutes or until well browned and puffed. Serve hot.

Makes about 24.
- Tartlets can be made 3 hours ahead.
- Storage: Covered, in refrigerator.
- Freeze: Cooked tartlets suitable.
- Microwave: Not suitable.

LEFT: Clockwise from back: Creamy Smoked Salmon Tartlets, Chicken Coconut Bites, Crispy Crab Triangles.

Plates from Barbara's House & Garden

CASHEW AND BASIL TARTLETS

**3 sheets ready rolled
   shortcrust pastry**
paprika

CASHEW FILLING
30g butter
1 onion, finely chopped
125g packet cream cheese
30g butter, extra
¼ cup roasted cashew nuts
2 tablespoons chopped fresh basil
1 egg yolk
¼ cup cream
¼ cup grated fresh parmesan cheese

Cut 5cm rounds from pastry, press into lightly greased mini muffin pans (1 tablespoon capacity), prick well with fork. Bake in moderately hot oven for about 10 minutes or until lightly browned, remove from pan to wire rack.

Just before serving, spoon filling into piping bag fitted with 1cm plain tube, pipe filling evenly into pastry cases. Place tartlets on oven tray, bake in moderate oven for about 10 minutes or until filling is set. Sprinkle lightly with paprika just before serving.

Cashew Filling: Heat butter in pan, add onion, cook, stirring, until onion is soft.

Blend or process remaining ingredients until smooth, stir in onion mixture.
   Makes about 60.
■ Pastry cases and filling can be prepared a day ahead.
■ Storage: Filling, in refrigerator. Pastry cases in airtight container.
■ Freeze: Pastry cases suitable.
■ Microwave: Not suitable.

LAMB KEBABS WITH AVOCADO APRICOT DIP

500g lamb fillets
2 tablespoons lime juice
1 clove garlic, crushed
1 tablespoon sugar
bay leaves
380g baby mushrooms

AVOCADO APRICOT DIP
1 large avocado, chopped
1 teaspoon Tabasco sauce
1 tablespoon sour cream
⅓ cup chopped dried apricots

Trim excess fat from lamb, cut lamb into 2cm pieces. Combine lamb, juice, garlic and sugar in bowl; cover, refrigerate several hours or overnight.

Thread lamb, bay leaves and mushrooms onto 15 skewers.

Just before serving, grill kebabs until browned and tender. Serve hot with dip.

Avocado Apricot Dip: Blend or process avocado, sauce and sour cream until smooth; stir in apricots.

Makes 15.

■ Kebabs can be prepared a day ahead; dip an hour ahead.
■ Storage: Both, covered, in refrigerator.
■ Freeze: Not suitable.
■ Microwave: Not suitable.

ABOVE: From left: Cashew and Basil Tartlets, Lamb Kebabs with Avocado Apricot Dip.

53

QUICK SAUSAGE ROLLS

2 cups self-raising flour
2 teaspoons castor sugar
20g butter
1 cup milk, approximately
20 (about 500g) chipolata sausages
1 egg, lightly beaten

Sift flour and sugar into bowl, rub in butter, stir in enough milk to mix to a soft dough. Turn dough onto lightly floured surface, knead gently until smooth. Roll dough on lightly floured surface until 3mm thick.

Cut dough into 8cm x 9cm rectangles, lightly brush edges with water. Roll sausages in rectangles of dough, pinching ends to seal.

Place sausage rolls onto greased oven trays, lightly brush with egg, cut 3 slits on top of each roll.

Just before serving, bake rolls in moderate oven for about 25 minutes or until browned. Cut sausage rolls in half before serving.

Makes about 40.

■ Can be prepared several hours ahead.
■ Storage: Covered, on oven tray.
■ Freeze: Cooked rolls suitable.
■ Microwave: Not suitable.

WARM CORN AND CHIVE DIP

250g jar corn relish
300g carton sour cream
few drops Tabasco sauce
2 tablespoons chopped fresh chives
½ cup grated tasty cheese

Combine all ingredients in pan, stir over heat until heated through; do not boil. Serve with corn chips.

Makes about 2 cups.

■ Dip can be prepared 1 day ahead.
■ Storage: Covered, in refrigerator.
■ Freeze: Not suitable.
■ Microwave: Suitable.

DEEP-FRIED MARINATED CHICKEN

500g chicken thigh fillets
2cm piece fresh ginger
2 teaspoons curry powder
½ teaspoon five spice powder
½ teaspoon ground cumin
2 cloves garlic, crushed
½ teaspoon sambal oelek
1 teaspoon sugar
1 teaspoon grated lime rind
¼ cup lime juice
cornflour
oil for deep-frying

Cut chicken into 2cm cubes. Grate ginger finely, press between 2 spoons over large bowl to extract juice; discard pulp. Stir in chicken, curry powder, spices, garlic, sambal oelek, sugar, rind and juice; cover, refrigerate several hours or overnight.

Just before serving, drain chicken, toss in cornflour, shake away excess cornflour. Deep-fry chicken in hot oil until browned and tender.

Makes about 30.

■ Can be prepared a day ahead.
■ Storage: Covered, in refrigerator.
■ Freeze: Uncooked chicken suitable.
■ Microwave: Not suitable.

LEFT: Clockwise from front: Warm Corn and Chive Dip, Quick Sausage Rolls, Deep-Fried Marinated Chicken.

China from Kenwick Galleries

SPICY LAMB IN RICE PAPER

2 (180g) lamb fillets, thinly sliced
1 clove garlic, crushed
1 teaspoon honey
1 teaspoon oil
3 teaspoons light soy sauce
pinch five spice powder
½ teaspoon grated fresh ginger
25 sheets rice paper
1 egg, lightly beaten
oil for deep-frying

Combine lamb, garlic, honey, oil, sauce, five spice powder and ginger in bowl; cover, refrigerate 30 minutes.

Cut rice paper in half crossways, brush a piece of rice paper with some egg. Place a piece of lamb at corner of paper, roll up and tuck ends in, press lightly to flatten. Repeat with remaining rice paper, egg and lamb.

Just before serving, deep-fry parcels in hot oil until crisp but not browned.

Makes about 50.

■ Can be prepared 2 hours ahead.
■ Storage: Covered, in refrigerator.
■ Freeze: Not suitable.
■ Microwave: Not suitable.

CREAMY TORTELLINI PICK-UPS

200g mixed tortellini
30g butter
1 clove garlic, crushed
¼ cup cream
¼ cup grated fresh parmesan cheese
2 tablespoons chopped fresh parsley

Add tortellini to large saucepan of boiling water, boil, uncovered, for about 15 minutes or until tender; drain.

Heat butter in pan, stir in garlic, cook 1 minute. Stir in cream, cheese and parsley, cook 1 minute. Add tortellini to pan; mix well.

Cool tortellini 5 minutes before threading onto toothpicks. Serve warm.

Makes about 25.

■ Tortellini can be prepared several hours ahead.
■ Storage: Covered, in refrigerator.
■ Freeze: Not suitable.
■ Microwave: Suitable.

SMOKED CHEESE AND MOZZARELLA BALLS

60g butter
3 green shallots, chopped
¼ cup plain flour
1 cup milk
½ cup grated mozzarella cheese
1 cup (85g) grated smoked cheese
1 tablespoon chopped fresh chives
½ cup plain flour, extra
oil for deep-frying

Heat butter in pan, add shallots, cook, stirring, until soft. Stir in flour, stir until bubbling. Remove from heat, gradually stir in milk, stir over heat until sauce boils and thickens. Combine cheeses, chives and extra flour in bowl, mix well, stir into hot sauce mixture; cool to room temperature.

Using floured hands, roll 2 level teaspoons of mixture into a ball, repeat with remaining mixture.

Just before serving, deep-fry balls in hot oil until golden brown, drain on absorbent paper. Serve hot.

Makes about 50.

■ Can be prepared several hours ahead.
■ Storage: At room temperature.
■ Freeze: Uncooked balls suitable.
■ Microwave: Not suitable.

RIGHT: Clockwise from right: Spicy Lamb in Rice Paper, Creamy Tortellini Pick-Ups, Smoked Cheese and Mozzarella Balls.

China from Limoges

SMOKED TROUT PIKELETS

½ cup self-raising flour
¼ cup wholemeal self-raising flour
1 egg, lightly beaten
⅔ cup milk
20g butter, melted
1 tablespoon chopped fresh chives
2 teaspoons chopped fresh dill
½ cup grated gruyere cheese
100g sliced smoked trout
1 tablespoon (25g) trout or
    salmon roe
fresh dill sprigs

Sift flours into bowl, gradually add egg and
milk, mix to a smooth batter. Stir in butter
and herbs. Drop level teaspoons of mixture into heated greased heavy-based
pan, cook until bubbles appear; turn
pikelets, brown other side.

Just before serving, top each pikelet
with a little cheese, grill until cheese is
melted. Top with trout, roe and dill.
    Makes about 50.
- ■ Can be made several hours ahead.
- ■ Storage: In airtight container.
- ■ Freeze: Pikelets suitable.
- ■ Microwave: Not suitable.

RATATOUILLE CRESCENTS

2 teaspoons olive oil
½ small onion, finely chopped
1 clove garlic, crushed
½ small eggplant, finely chopped
½ zucchini, finely chopped
½ x 410g can tomatoes
¼ teaspoon sugar
1 tablespoon chopped fresh parsley
2 teaspoons chopped fresh basil
2 sheets ready rolled puff pastry
1 egg, lightly beaten
2 tablespoons grated parmesan
    cheese

Heat oil in pan, add onion and garlic, cook,
stirring, until onion is soft. Stir in
eggplant and zucchini, stir until
vegetables are soft. Stir in undrained
crushed tomatoes and sugar, bring to boil,
simmer, uncovered, for about 20 minutes
or until most of the liquid has evaporated.
Stir in herbs; cool to room temperature.

    Cut pastry into 5cm squares, top each
square with 1 level teaspoon of eggplant
mixture. Lightly brush edges of pastry with
water, fold pastry in half diagonally, press
edges with a fork. Bend triangles to form
crescents. Place crescents on lightly
greased oven tray, lightly brush with egg,
sprinkle with cheese.

Just before serving, bake crescents in
moderate oven for about 15 minutes or
until lightly browned.
    Makes about 50.
- ■ Can be prepared a day ahead.
- ■ Storage: Covered, in refrigerator.
- ■ Freeze: Uncooked crescents suitable.
- ■ Microwave: Not suitable.

CHICKEN CHEESE PATTIES

1 tablespoon oil
1 onion, chopped
1 teaspoon curry powder
½ teaspoon grated fresh ginger
500g minced chicken
2 teaspoons French mustard
2 tablespoons chopped fresh chives
1 cup (100g) stale breadcrumbs
packaged breadcrumbs
oil for shallow-frying
60g Jarlsberg cheese, chopped

Heat oil in pan, add onion, curry powder and ginger, cook, stirring, until onion is soft. Combine onion mixture, chicken, mustard, chives and stale breadcrumbs in bowl. Roll 2 level teaspoons of mixture into a ball, toss in packaged breadcrumbs, flatten slightly, place onto toothpick. Repeat with remaining mixture and breadcrumbs; cover, refrigerate 1 hour.

Shallow-fry patties in hot oil until well browned and cooked through; drain on absorbent paper.

Just before serving, top each patty with a piece of cheese, grill until cheese is melted and lightly browned.

Makes about 45.

■ Patties can be prepared a day ahead.
■ Storage: Covered, in refrigerator.
■ Freeze: Cooked patties suitable.
■ Microwave: Not suitable.

LEFT: Clockwise from front: Smoked Trout Pikelets, Ratatouille Crescents, Chicken Cheese Patties.

CHEESE FONDUE WITH CRUNCHY RYE CUBES

3 teaspoons drained canned green peppercorns
2 cups dry white wine
1 clove garlic, crushed
3⅓ cups (400g) grated gruyere cheese
2¼ cups (250g) grated Swiss cheese
1 cup (125g) grated tasty cheese
¼ cup plain flour
CRUNCHY RYE CUBES
900g loaf unsliced black rye bread
60g butter, melted
1 teaspoon dried rosemary, crushed

Combine peppercorns, wine and garlic in pan, bring to boil, simmer, uncovered, for 2 minutes; remove from heat, stand mixture for 1 hour.
Just before serving, heat wine mixture in pan, stir in well combined cheeses and flour, stir over heat until mixture starts bubbling. Remove from heat, serve with crunchy rye cubes.

Crunchy Rye Cubes: Cut bread into 1½cm cubes. Combine butter and rosemary in bowl, add cubes, toss well. Place cubes on oven tray, bake in moderate oven for 10 minutes, turn cubes, bake further 10 minutes or until crunchy; drain on absorbent paper.

Makes about 4 cups fondue.
■ Rye cubes can be made a day ahead.
■ Storage: Cubes in airtight container.
■ Freeze: Uncooked rye cubes suitable.
■ Microwave: Not suitable.

PRAWN AND PORK WONTONS

125g small cooked shelled prawns
250g pork mince
2 green shallots, chopped
1 egg, separated
1 tablespoon dark soy sauce
½ teaspoon sesame oil
60 egg pastry sheets
oil for deep-frying

Chop prawns, combine with mince, shallots, egg yolk, sauce and oil in bowl. Place 1 level teaspoon of prawn mixture on centre of each pastry sheet. Brush edges of sheets lightly with egg white, pleat edges, bring together in centre, press firmly to seal.
Just before serving, deep-fry wontons in hot oil until lightly browned and cooked through. (Wontons can also be cooked in pan of boiling water for about 3 minutes or until cooked through.) Drain on absorbent paper. Serve hot.

Makes 60.
■ Can be prepared 6 hours ahead.
■ Storage: Covered, in refrigerator.
■ Freeze: Uncooked wontons suitable.
■ Microwave: Not suitable.

BELOW: From left: Cheese Fondue with Crunchy Rye Cubes, Prawn and Pork Wontons.
RIGHT: From left: Crispy Beef Strips in Nutty Oat Crumbs, Baby Potatoes with Caraway Carrot Filling.

Below: Plate from Oceanfront Galleries

BABY POTATOES WITH CARAWAY CARROT FILLING

**20 (600g) baby new potatoes,
  unpeeled**
2 medium (200g) carrots, chopped
¼ cup sour cream
1 teaspoon caraway seeds
2 teaspoons chopped fresh chives
2 teaspoons lemon juice
**2 tablespoons chopped fresh
  chives, extra**

Boil, steam or microwave potatoes and carrots until tender, drain; cool. Blend or process carrots until smooth.

Cut tops from potatoes; discard tops. Carefully scoop out flesh from potatoes, mash flesh in bowl. Add quarter of the flesh to carrot; mix well. (Keep remaining potato for another use.) Stir in sour cream, seeds, chives and juice. Spoon carrot mixture into potatoes, sprinkle with extra chives, place on oven tray.

Just before serving, heat potatoes in moderate oven for about 10 minutes.
  Makes 20.
■ Can be prepared a day ahead.
■ Storage: Covered, in refrigerator.
■ Freeze: Not suitable.
■ Microwave: Suitable.

CRISPY BEEF STRIPS IN NUTTY OAT CRUMBS

2 tablespoons brown sugar
⅔ cup Crunchy Oat-Bran cereal
½ cup unsalted roasted peanuts
½ teaspoon ground coriander
½ teaspoon grated lime rind
250g piece rump steak
plain flour
1 egg, lightly beaten
oil for deep-frying
¼ cup lime juice

Blend or process sugar, cereal, nuts, coriander and rind until fine, transfer to bowl. Cut steak into thin strips, toss in flour, shake away excess flour, dip into egg, then cereal mixture.

Just before serving, deep-fry strips in hot oil until crisp. Serve hot, drizzled with lime juice.
  Makes about 30.
■ Strips can be prepared a day ahead.
■ Storage: Covered, in refrigerator.
■ Freeze: Uncooked strips suitable.
■ Microwave: Not suitable.

CORNMEAL AND SALMON MUFFINS

1 cup cornmeal
½ cup self-raising flour
2 tablespoons castor sugar
1 egg
1 cup buttermilk
2 eggs, extra
½ cup cream
210g can salmon, drained, flaked
130g can corn kernels, drained

Combine cornmeal, sifted flour and sugar in bowl. Stir in combined egg and buttermilk; mix well. Whisk extra eggs and cream in another bowl until combined, stir in salmon and corn.

Spoon 1½ level teaspoons of cornmeal mixture into 1 hole of greased mini muffin pans (1 tablespoon capacity), top with 1½ level teaspoons of salmon mixture. Repeat with remaining mixtures. Bake in moderately hot oven for about 12 minutes or until muffins are lightly browned. Serve muffins hot.

Makes about 55.
■ Muffins can be made 3 hours ahead.
■ Storage: Covered, on oven tray.
■ Freeze: Suitable.
■ Microwave: Not suitable.

CHICKEN AND ASPARAGUS PASTRIES

4 sheets ready rolled puff pastry
1 cup (150g) chopped cooked chicken
½ cup chopped cooked or drained
    canned asparagus
2 tablespoons sour cream
2 tablespoons chopped fresh chives
50g tasty cheese, finely chopped
1 egg, lightly beaten

Cut each pastry sheet into 4 strips, cut each strip crossways to give 3 rectangles. Roll each rectangle on lightly floured surface to an 8cm x 10cm rectangle.

Combine chicken, asparagus, sour cream, chives and cheese in bowl. Spoon a level teaspoon of mixture onto each pastry rectangle, lightly brush edges with egg, fold in long sides, fold in ends. Place pastries seam side down on greased oven trays.

Just before serving, brush pastries with egg, bake in moderately hot oven for about 15 minutes or until lightly browned.

Makes 48.
■ Can be prepared 3 hours ahead.
■ Storage: Covered, in refrigerator.
■ Freeze: Cooked pastries suitable.
■ Microwave: Not suitable.

LEFT: From front: Chicken and Asparagus Pastries, Cornmeal and Salmon Muffins.

China from Limoges

HERBED CHEESES
IN GOLDEN BREAD CASES

1 loaf unsliced white bread
90g butter, melted
¼ cup grated gruyere cheese

FILLING
40g butter
2½ tablespoons plain flour
1¼ cups milk
1 egg yolk
⅔ cup grated gruyere cheese
⅔ cup grated fresh parmesan cheese
1 teaspoon chopped fresh chives
1 teaspoon chopped fresh basil
1 teaspoon chopped fresh oregano

Cut bread crossways into 3cm slices, remove crusts. Cut slices into 3 strips, cut each strip crossways in half to make 3cm x 5cm rectangles. Scoop centres from rectangles, leaving 8mm shells. Brush rim and edges of shells with butter, place on oven tray, bake in moderate oven for about 15 minutes or until lightly browned. Spoon filling into cases, sprinkle with grated gruyere cheese.

Just before serving, heat cheese cases in moderate oven for about 10 minutes.

Filling: Heat butter in pan, stir in flour, cook until bubbling. Remove from heat, gradually stir in milk, stir over heat until mixture boils and thickens. Remove from heat, stir in egg yolk and cheeses, stir over low heat until smooth; stir in herbs.

Makes about 36.
- Bread cases can be made a day ahead; filling an hour ahead.
- Storage: Bread cases in airtight container. Filling at room temperature.
- Freeze: Not suitable.
- Microwave: Not suitable.

GINGERED LAMB TURNOVERS

1½ cups plain flour
¾ cup boiling water
1 egg white, lightly beaten
oil for deep-frying

FILLING
1 tablespoon oil
1 clove garlic, crushed
2 teaspoons grated fresh ginger
½ teaspoon ground coriander
250g minced lamb
4 green shallots, chopped
1 tablespoon dark soy sauce

Sift flour into bowl, stir in boiling water, mix to a firm dough. Knead dough gently on lightly floured surface until smooth; cover, stand 15 minutes.

Roll half the dough on lightly floured surface until 2mm thick, cut 8cm rounds from dough. Repeat with remaining dough. Place 1 level teaspoon of filling on each round, brush edges lightly with egg white, fold rounds in half, press edges together to seal.

Just before serving, deep-fry turnovers in hot oil until well browned and heated through; drain on absorbent paper.

Filling: Heat oil in pan, add garlic, ginger

and coriander, cook for 1 minute. Add lamb, cook, stirring, for about 5 minutes or until well browned. Stir in shallots and sauce; cool.

Makes about 36.
- Can be prepared a day ahead.
- Storage: Covered, in refrigerator.
- Freeze: Uncooked turnovers suitable.
- Microwave: Not suitable.

PORK AND VEAL ROLLS
IN CRISP NOODLE CRUMBS

300g pork and veal mince
2 cloves garlic, crushed
1 teaspoon grated fresh ginger
½ teaspoon ground cumin
½ teaspoon ground coriander
1 small fresh red chilli, chopped
2 green shallots, chopped
¼ cup canned drained water
**   chestnuts, chopped**
1 egg white, lightly beaten
2 teaspoons cornflour
2 teaspoons light soy sauce
¼ teaspoon sesame oil
250g fresh egg noodles, chopped
oil for deep-frying

Combine all ingredients except noodles and oil for deep-frying in bowl. Roll 2 level teaspoons of mixture into a log shape, roll in noodles. Repeat with remaining mixture and noodles.

Just before serving, deep-fry rolls in hot oil until well browned and cooked through; drain on absorbent paper.

Makes about 25.
- Rolls can be prepared 2 days ahead.
- Storage: Covered, in refrigerator.
- Freeze: Uncooked rolls suitable.
- Microwave: Not suitable.

RIGHT: Clockwise from left: Herbed Cheeses in Golden Bread Cases, Gingered Lamb Turnovers, Pork and Veal Rolls in Crisp Noodle Crumbs.

Plates from Accoutrement

Cold Savouries

Some of these tempting appetisers are cooked, some are uncooked, and all are served cold. Some can be made entirely in advance; others are completed just before serving. They make an easy start to your party and, while they are being served, you have the chance to cook (or finish) the hot savouries you've planned. When preparing or making ahead, keep food well covered with plastic wrap in the refrigerator or airtight container, as indicated in recipes; it is important to exclude as much air as possible. Some of these savouries benefit from being served at room temperature; see recipes.

EGG AND TOMATO PICKS WITH GARLIC MAYONNAISE

24 quail eggs
250g punnet small cherry
    tomatoes, halved
1 bunch fresh basil

GARLIC MAYONNAISE
1 egg
1 egg yolk
1 tablespoon lemon juice
1 cup oil
1 tablespoon chopped fresh chives
1 clove garlic, crushed

Place quail eggs in pan, cover with cold water, bring to boil, simmer, uncovered, for 3 minutes. Drain eggs, rinse under cold water; cool, remove shells.

Cut eggs in half, thread eggs, tomatoes and basil leaves onto toothpicks. Serve with garlic mayonnaise.

Garlic Mayonnaise: Blend or process egg, egg yolk and juice until smooth. With motor operating, gradually add oil in thin stream, blend until thickened. Stir in chives and garlic.

Makes 48.
- Can be made 3 hours ahead.
- Storage: Covered, in refrigerator.
- Freeze: Not suitable.
- Microwave: Not suitable.

MEATBALLS IN CHEESY PASTRY

1 cup plain flour
pinch cayenne pepper
100g butter
1¼ cups (150g) grated tasty cheese
1 egg, lightly beaten
2 tablespoons sesame seeds

MEATBALLS
250g minced beef
1 teaspoon grated lime rind
1 tablespoon lime juice

Process flour, pepper and butter until combined. Add cheese, process until mixture forms a ball. Knead dough on lightly floured surface until smooth; cover, refrigerate 30 minutes.

Roll pastry between sheets of greaseproof paper until 2mm thick. Cut 4cm rounds from pastry, top each round with a meatball. Fold pastry around to enclose meatballs completely, roll into balls. Brush tops with egg, sprinkle with seeds, place about 3cm apart on greased oven trays. Cover, refrigerate 30 minutes.

Bake pastry-covered meatballs in moderately hot oven about 15 minutes or until lightly browned; cool before serving.

Meatballs: Combine all ingredients in bowl; mix well. Roll level teaspoons of mixture into balls.

Makes about 45.
- Can be made 3 hours ahead.
- Storage: Covered, in refrigerator.
- Freeze: Cooked meatballs suitable.
- Microwave: Not suitable.

SMOKED TROUT WITH CREME FRAICHE

1 medium (100g) potato, finely
    chopped
2 tablespoons mayonnaise
200g sliced smoked trout
1 bunch (about 20) chives

CREME FRAICHE
½ cup thickened cream
½ cup sour cream

Boil, steam or microwave potato until tender, drain. Combine potato and mayonnaise in bowl while still hot; cool.

Spoon potato mixture onto trout slices, fold in sides and roll up to form parcels.

Drop chives in pan of boiling water; drain immediately. Tie each parcel with a chive, trim chive ends; serve with creme friache.

Creme Fraiche: Combine creams in bowl, cover, leave at room temperature until thick; this will take 1 or 2 days, depending on weather. Refrigerate until required.

Makes about 20.
- Parcels can be made 6 hours ahead; creme fraiche a week ahead.
- Storage: Both, covered, in refrigerator.
- Freeze: Not suitable.
- Microwave: Potato suitable.

RIGHT: From back: Egg and Tomato Picks with Garlic Mayonnaise, Meatballs in Cheesy Pastry, Smoked Trout with Creme Fraiche.

Plates from Mikasa

CREAMY PRAWNS IN NOODLE NESTS

1 bacon rasher, chopped
2 tablespoons sour cream
100g fresh egg noodles
2 tablespoons oil
24 small cooked prawns, shelled
1 tablespoon alfalfa sprouts

Cook bacon in pan until crisp; cool. Combine bacon with sour cream.

Place egg noodles in bowl, cover with hot water, stand 5 minutes; drain well. Divide noodles evenly between 24 oiled mini muffin pans (1 tablespoon capacity), press firmly into pans, brush lightly and evenly with oil. Bake in moderate oven for about 15 minutes or until crisp.

Remove nests from pans with metal spatula, place upside down on wire rack, place rack on oven tray, return to oven for about 5 minutes or until nests are crisp; cool to room temperature.

Just before serving, top each nest with a prawn, sour cream mixture and sprouts.

Makes 24.

- Nests can be made 3 days ahead.
- Storage: In airtight container.
- Freeze: Nests suitable.
- Microwave: Not suitable.

SPICY SOUR CREAM SCONES

1¼ cups self-raising flour
¼ teaspoon turmeric
½ teaspoon curry powder
30g butter
¼ teaspoon fennel seeds
1 green shallot, chopped
½ cup sour cream
¼ cup milk, approximately
300g carton sour cream, extra
fresh fennel sprigs

Sift dry ingredients into bowl, rub in butter, stir in seeds, shallot, sour cream and enough milk to mix to a firm dough. Knead dough on lightly floured surface until smooth, roll dough until 1cm thick. Cut into 3½cm rounds, place on greased oven tray. Bake in hot oven for about 12 minutes or until scones are lightly browned and sound hollow when tapped on bases; cool on wire rack.

Just before serving, break scones in half, sandwich with extra sour cream and fennel sprigs.

Makes about 45.

- Scones can be made 3 hours ahead.
- Storage: In airtight container.
- Freeze: Unfilled scones suitable.
- Microwave: Not suitable.

BARBECUED PORK ON RICE CRACKERS

½ x 100g packet plain rice crackers
200g piece Chinese barbecued pork, sliced
1 tablespoon hoisin sauce
½ teaspoon water
2 tablespoons canned drained water chestnuts, chopped
2 green shallots, chopped

Top each rice cracker with pork. Place combined sauce and water into small piping bag fitted with small plain tube, pipe thin lines over pork. Top with water chestnuts and shallots.

Makes about 30.

- Can be made 30 minutes ahead.
- Storage: Covered, in refrigerator.
- Freeze: Not suitable.

LEFT: Creamy Prawns in Noodle Nests.
ABOVE: From left: Spicy Sour Cream Scones, Barbecued Pork on Rice Crackers.

Left: Bowl from Accoutrement. Above: Lacquered mat from Made in Japan

SMOKED TROUT AND AVOCADO FINGERS

½ (125g) smoked trout, skinned, boned
½ large avocado, chopped
1 tablespoon lemon juice
2 tablespoons sour cream
¼ teaspoon lemon pepper
¼ teaspoon horseradish cream
8 slices white bread
60g butter, softened

Blend or process trout, avocado, juice, cream, pepper and horseradish until smooth; cover, refrigerate several hours.

Remove and discard crusts from bread, butter each side of bread, cut each slice in half, then each half into 4 fingers. Place bread on oven tray, bake in moderate oven for 6 minutes, turn bread over, bake further 6 minutes or until lightly browned; cool. Spoon trout mixture into piping bag fitted with small fluted tube, pipe mixture onto toast fingers.

Makes 64.
■ Fingers can be made 4 hours ahead.
■ Storage: Covered, in refrigerator.
■ Freeze: Toast fingers suitable.
■ Microwave: Not suitable.

CURRIED PEPITAS AND MACADAMIAS

2 tablespoons oil
1 tablespoon curry powder
½ teaspoon rock salt
¾ cup pepitas
1¼ cups (175g) macadamias

Combine oil and curry powder in baking dish, stir over heat for about 2 minutes, or until fragrant. Add salt, pepitas and nuts, stir until coated with oil. Bake in moderate oven for about 10 minutes or until lightly browned, stirring occasionally; cool.

Makes about 2 cups.
■ Recipe can be made 3 weeks ahead.
■ Storage: In airtight container.
■ Freeze: Suitable.
■ Microwave: Not suitable.

GREEN OLIVES IN HERB AND ONION MARINADE

500g green olives, pitted
1 small onion, finely chopped
1 stick celery, finely chopped
¼ cup olive oil
¼ cup white vinegar
pinch chilli powder
1½ tablespoons chopped fresh basil
2 teaspoons chopped fresh oregano
2 teaspoons chopped fresh chives

Combine all ingredients in bowl; refrigerate overnight.

Makes about 2 cups.
■ Olives can be made a month ahead.
■ Storage: Covered, in refrigerator.
■ Freeze: Not suitable.

ORANGE AND SMOKED TURKEY CUBES

125g packet cream cheese
pinch paprika
9 slices white bread
150g sliced smoked turkey
½ avocado, mashed
1 orange, segmented

Beat cheese and paprika in bowl with electric mixer until smooth. Spread 3 bread slices with some cheese mixture, top with a layer of turkey, then spread thinly with avocado. Spread another 3 slices of bread with cheese mixture, place cheese side down on previous slices. Repeat spreading and layering with remaining cheese mixture, turkey, avocado and bread. Cut crusts from sandwiches, cut sandwiches into 3 fingers, cut fingers into 3 cubes. Toothpick a small piece of orange onto each cube.

Makes 27.
■ Cubes can be made 2 hours ahead.
■ Storage: Covered, in refrigerator.
■ Freeze: Not suitable.

ABOVE: Orange and Smoked Turkey Cubes.
RIGHT: Clockwise from top: Curried Pepitas and Macadamias, Smoked Trout and Avocado Fingers, Green Olives in Herb and Onion Marinade.

Right: Plates from Oceanfront Galleries

PASTRAMI HORSERADISH CONES

1 sheet ready rolled puff pastry
1 egg white, lightly beaten
PASTRAMI HORSERADISH FILLING
1 egg yolk
1 teaspoon white vinegar
3 teaspoons horseradish cream
½ cup oil
6 slices pastrami, chopped
2 gherkins, chopped

Lightly grease small cream horn moulds.

Cut pastry into 1cm strips, cut each strip in half crossways. Brush each strip lightly with egg white. Starting at point of each mould, wind pastry strips, egg white side out, around moulds, overlapping edges of pastry slightly.

Place cones on lightly greased oven tray, seam side down, brush lightly with egg white. Bake in hot oven for 5 minutes, reduce heat to moderate, bake further 8 minutes or until cones are browned and crisp. Remove cones from moulds, cool on wire rack. Repeat with remaining pastry and egg white.

Just before serving, fill cones with filling.
Pastrami Horseradish Filling: Blend or process yolk, vinegar and horseradish cream until smooth. Add oil gradually in thin stream while motor is operating, blend until thickened. Stir in pastrami and gherkins, refrigerate 1 hour.

Makes about 50.
- Cones and filling can be made separately 2 days ahead.
- Storage: Cones, in airtight container. Filling, covered, in refrigerator.
- Freeze: Unfilled cones suitable.
- Microwave: Not suitable.

POPPYSEED CRACKERS WITH TWO DIPS

1 cup self-raising flour
¾ cup plain flour
2 teaspoons poppy seeds
2 teaspoons dried oregano leaves
1 teaspoon ground black peppercorns
½ teaspoon chilli powder
2 tablespoons tomato paste
2 tablespoons oil
½ cup water
TOMATO DIP
1 tomato, finely chopped
2 green shallots, chopped
1 small onion, finely chopped
1 tablespoon chopped fresh mint
1 tablespoon white vinegar

SOUR CREAM DIP
300g carton sour cream
1 tablespoon lemon juice
1 tablespoon chopped fresh dill

Sift flours into bowl, stir in seeds, oregano, pepper and chilli, then combined paste, oil and water, mix to a firm dough. Knead dough on lightly floured surface; cover, refrigerate 30 minutes.

Roll out dough on lightly floured surface until 3mm thick. Cut 5½cm rounds from dough. Place rounds on greased oven trays, bake in moderate oven for about 15 minutes or until lightly browned; cool on wire racks. Serve crackers with dips.

Tomato Dip: Squeeze excess moisture from tomato, combine in bowl with remaining ingredients.
Sour Cream Dip: Combine all ingredients in bowl, mix well.

Makes about 80 crackers.
- Crackers can be made a week ahead. Dips can be made a day ahead.
- Storage: Crackers, in airtight container. Dips, covered, in refrigerator.
- Freeze: Not suitable.
- Microwave: Not suitable.

LEFT: Pastrami Horseradish Cones.
ABOVE: Poppyseed Crackers with Two Dips.

Left: China from Limoges

73

PESTO DIP WITH CRISP GARLIC WEDGES

1 cup chopped fresh basil
1 clove garlic, crushed
2 tablespoons pine nuts, toasted
2 tablespoons grated fresh
  parmesan cheese
2 tablespoons olive oil
2 teaspoons lemon juice
300g carton sour cream
CRISP GARLIC WEDGES
4 rounds pita bread
150g butter, melted
2 cloves garlic, crushed
⅔ cup grated fresh parmesan cheese

Blend or process basil, garlic, nuts, cheese, oil and juice until smooth. Combine in bowl with sour cream; serve with crisp garlic wedges.

Crisp Garlic Wedges: Split bread rounds in half, cut into large wedges, place split side up on oven trays. Brush with combined butter and garlic, sprinkle with cheese. Bake in moderately hot oven for about 8 minutes or until lightly browned and crisp.

■ Both can be made a day ahead.
■ Storage: Dip, covered, in refrigerator. Wedges, in airtight container.
■ Freeze: Wedges suitable.
■ Microwave: Not suitable.

CHEESY HAM AND MELON BALLS

340g can leg ham, chopped
250g packet cream cheese, chopped
1 tablespoon orange marmalade
2 teaspoons ground ginger
¾ cup sesame seeds, toasted
1 rockmelon

Process ham until finely chopped, add cheese, marmalade and ginger, process until smooth. Transfer mixture to bowl; cover, refrigerate 1 hour or until firm.

Shape 1½ level teaspoons of mixture into balls, toss in seeds, place on tray, refrigerate until firm. Using a melon baller, scoop balls from rockmelon.

Just before serving, thread cheesy ham balls and rockmelon balls onto toothpicks.

Makes about 50.

- Recipe can be prepared a day ahead.
- Storage: Covered, in refrigerator.
- Freeze: Not suitable.

BEEF CROUTES
WITH MUSTARD MAYONNAISE

500g piece beef fillet
2 tablespoons oil
2 small French bread sticks
20g butter, melted
1 tablespoon oil, extra
fresh tarragon

MUSTARD MAYONNAISE
½ cup mayonnaise
3 teaspoons seeded mustard
1 tablespoon chopped fresh tarragon

Secure beef with string at 3cm intervals. Heat oil in baking dish, add beef, cook until well browned all over. Bake in dish in hot oven for about 15 minutes or until beef is done as desired; cool.

Cut bread into 1cm slices, brush with combined butter and extra oil, place on oven tray. Bake in moderate oven for about 5 minutes or until lightly browned and crisp; cool. Cut beef into thin slices.

Just before serving, top bread with beef, mayonnaise and tarragon.

Mustard Mayonnaise: Combine all ingredients in bowl.

Makes about 40.

- Beef, bread and mayonnaise can be prepared separately a day ahead.
- Storage: Beef and mayonnaise, covered, in refrigerator. Bread, in airtight container.
- Freeze: Bread suitable.
- Microwave: Not suitable.

LEFT: Pesto Dip with Crisp Garlic Wedges.
ABOVE: From left: Beef Croutes with Mustard Mayonnaise, Cheesy Ham and Melon Balls.
Left: Plate and bowl from Something Special

NUTTY NIBBLE MIX

2½ cups (100g) Nutri-Grain
    breakfast cereal
200g packet soya crisps
⅓ cup unroasted unsalted peanuts
⅓ cup unroasted unsalted
    cashews
⅓ cup almond kernels
⅓ cup unsalted macadamias
⅔ cup pepitas
¼ cup olive oil
125g butter
3 teaspoons ground cumin
1 teaspoon ground coriander
¼ teaspoon ground cardamom
1½ teaspoons garam masala
½ teaspoon garlic powder
2 teaspoons celery salt
½ teaspoon ground black pepper

Combine Nutri-Grain, crisps, nuts and pepitas in large bowl. Heat oil and butter in pan, stir in spices, salt and pepper, stir until foaming, pour over cereal mixture; mix well. Spread mixture on 2 oven trays in single layer, bake in moderately slow oven for about 35 minutes or until mix has dried out. Cool on trays.
    Makes about 4½ cups.
■ Mix can be made 1 month ahead.
■ Storage: In airtight container.
■ Freeze: Not suitable.
■ Microwave: Not suitable.

ABOVE: From front: Smoked Turkey and Cranberry Rounds, Nutty Nibble Mix.
RIGHT: From front: Cucumber Rounds with Herbed Cream Cheese, Roast Beef and Avocado on Pumpernickel.

Above: China from Limoges. Right: Plates from Made in Japan

SMOKED TURKEY AND CRANBERRY ROUNDS

3 large cabbage leaves
300g ricotta cheese
300g sliced smoked turkey breast
⅓ cup cranberry sauce
watercress sprigs

Spread leaves with cheese, top with turkey slices. Cut into 3½cm rounds.
Just before serving, top rounds with sauce and watercress.
    Makes about 65.
■ Rounds can be prepared a day ahead.
■ Storage: Covered, in refrigerator.
■ Freeze: Not suitable.

CUCUMBER ROUNDS WITH HERBED CREAM CHEESE

125g packet cream cheese
1 tablespoon sour cream
1 tablespoon chopped fresh basil
1 tablespoon chopped fresh parsley
1 teaspoon chopped fresh oregano
1/4 teaspoon chopped fresh rosemary
2 green shallots, chopped
1 teaspoon lemon juice
1 long green cucumber
fresh oregano sprigs, extra

Blend or process cheese, cream, herbs, shallots and juice until smooth. Cut cucumber into 5mm slices, top with cheese mixture, then extra oregano and pieces of red pepper, if desired. Cover, refrigerate for 2 hours.

Makes about 20.
■ Rounds can be made 3 hours ahead.
■ Storage: Covered, in refrigerator.
■ Freeze: Not suitable.

ROAST BEEF AND AVOCADO ON PUMPERNICKEL

100g packaged cream cheese
1/4 avocado, mashed
1 teaspoon lemon juice
1/4 small red pepper, finely chopped
180g sliced roast beef
125g butter
1 tablespoon chopped fresh parsley
250g packet sliced pumpernickel
    rounds
fresh parsley sprigs, extra

Beat cheese, avocado and half the juice in bowl with electric mixer until well combined; stir in pepper. Spread cheese mixture over beef slices, roll slices tightly; cover, refrigerate until firm. Cut beef rolls into 5mm slices diagonally.

Beat butter, parsley and remaining juice in bowl until smooth. Spoon mixture into piping bag fitted with fluted tube. Pipe swirls of butter mixture onto pumpernickel rounds, top with beef roll slices and extra parsley sprigs.

Makes about 24.
■ Rolls can be made 3 hours ahead.
■ Storage: Covered, in refrigerator.
■ Freeze: Not suitable.

OYSTERS WITH RED PEPPER DRESSING

40 oysters in shells
1 red pepper
½ cup oil
2 tablespoons lemon juice
1 teaspoon grated fresh ginger
1 tablespoon chopped fresh dill
2 teaspoons sour cream
fresh dill sprigs, extra

Remove oysters from shells, wash and dry shells; drain oysters on absorbent paper. Quarter pepper, remove seeds and membrane. Grill pepper, skin side up, until skin blisters. Peel skin, chop three-quarters of the pepper. Cut remaining pepper into thin strips; reserve strips. Blend or process chopped pepper, oil, juice, ginger, dill and sour cream until smooth. Combine mixture with oysters in bowl; cover, refrigerate 2 hours.

Just before serving, return oysters to shells, top with a little of the dressing, extra dill and reserved pepper.

Makes 40.
■ Oysters and dressing can be prepared a day ahead.
■ Storage: Covered, in refrigerator.
■ Freeze: Not suitable.
■ Microwave: Not suitable.

EGG AND HORSERADISH PUFFS

100g butter
1 cup water
1 cup plain flour
4 eggs, lightly beaten
FILLING
150g ricotta cheese
5 hard-boiled eggs
1½ teaspoons horseradish cream
½ teaspoon paprika
¼ teaspoon lemon juice

Combine butter and water in pan, bring to boil, stirring, until butter is melted. Add sifted flour all at once, stir vigorously over heat until mixture leaves side of pan and forms a smooth ball. Place mixture in bowl of electric mixer or processor. Add eggs gradually, beating well after each addition.

Spoon mixture into piping bag fitted with star tube, pipe 5cm lengths about 2cm apart onto lightly greased oven trays. Bake in moderate oven for about 20 minutes or until lightly browned and crisp; cool.

Just before serving, cut puffs in half, pipe or spoon filling into centres.

Filling: Blend or process all ingredients until smooth.

Makes about 35.
■ Puffs and filling can be made a day ahead separately.
■ Storage: Puffs, in airtight container. Filling, covered, in refrigerator.
■ Freeze: Unfilled puffs suitable.
■ Microwave: Not suitable.

THYME CRISPS

We had best results using a mortar and pestle, but thyme and salt can be crushed and chopped together.

10 x 10cm square egg pastry sheets
2 teaspoons chopped fresh thyme
1 teaspoon coarse cooking salt
oil for deep-frying

Cut pastry sheets in half, cut halves crossways into 2cm strips. Grind thyme and salt together using mortar and pestle. Deep-fry pastry strips in hot oil for about 5 seconds or until lightly browned; drain on absorbent paper. Sprinkle with thyme mixture; cool before serving.

Makes about 100.
■ Crisps can be made 2 weeks ahead.
■ Storage: In airtight container.
■ Freeze: Not suitable.
■ Microwave: Not suitable.

LEFT: Clockwise from front: Thyme Crisps, Egg and Horseradish Puffs, Oysters with Red Pepper Dressing.

China from Limoges

BLUE CHEESE APRICOT SWIRLS

100g blue vein cheese
100g packaged cream cheese
½ teaspoon canned drained green
 peppercorns, crushed
2 teaspoons chopped fresh basil
24 (130g) dried apricot halves
6 pitted black olives

Beat cheeses in bowl with electric mixer until smooth, beat in peppercorns and basil. Spoon mixture into piping bag fitted with fluted tube, pipe swirls of mixture onto apricots. Cut olives into slivers, top each swirl with 2 olive slivers.
 Makes 24.
■ Recipe can be made 3 hours ahead.
■ Storage: Covered, in refrigerator.
■ Freeze: Not suitable.

CHICKEN PEARL BALLS WITH MANGO SAUCE

400g minced chicken
1 tablespoon hoisin sauce
1 tablespoon light soy sauce
¼ teaspoon five spice powder
½ teaspoon sesame oil
½ cup stale breadcrumbs
1½ cups uncooked long grain rice

MANGO SAUCE
1 mango, chopped
2 tablespoons plain yogurt
1 tablespoon water
pinch five spice powder

Combine chicken, sauces, spice powder, oil and breadcrumbs in bowl. Toss 2 level teaspoons of mixture into rice, shape into a ball. Repeat with remaining mixture and rice. Place balls in single layer in top half of steamer, cook, covered, over simmering water for about 40 minutes or until rice is tender; cool before serving with sauce.
Sauce: Blend or process mango, yogurt, water and spice powder until smooth.
 Makes about 30.
■ Chicken balls and sauce can be made
 a day ahead.
■ Storage: Covered, in refrigerator.
■ Freeze: Chicken balls suitable.
■ Microwave: Not suitable.

LEEK AND MUSTARD PIES

3 cups plain flour
150g butter
1 egg
⅔ cup water, approximately
1 egg, lightly beaten, extra
FILLING
1 large (400g) leek, roughly chopped
1 carrot, roughly chopped
100g butter
¼ cup cream
1 tablespoon seeded mustard

Sift flour into bowl, rub in butter, add egg and enough water to mix to a firm dough. Knead dough on floured surface until smooth; cover, refrigerate 30 minutes.
 Roll half the pastry on lightly floured surface until 5mm thick, cut into 9cm rounds. Place rounds into greased deep 12-hole patty pan trays, spoon in filling, lightly brush pastry edges with extra egg.
 Roll out remaining pastry, cut 7½cm rounds from pastry, cut a small hole in centre of each round. Place rounds over filling, press edges of pastry to seal; brush tops with more extra egg. Bake pies in moderate oven for about 35 minutes or until well browned; cool on wire racks.
Just before serving, cut pies into quarters, serve at room temperature.
Filling: Process leek until finely chopped. Process carrot separately until finely chopped. Heat butter in pan, add leek and carrot, cook, stirring, until carrot is soft. Stir in cream and mustard, cook, uncovered, for about 10 minutes or until thick; cool.
 Makes 60.
■ Pies can be made a day ahead.
■ Storage: Covered, in refrigerator.
■ Freeze: Not suitable.
■ Microwave: Not suitable.

RIGHT: Clockwise from right: Leek and Mustard Pies, Blue Cheese Apricot Swirls, Chicken Pearl Balls with Mango Sauce.

CHICKEN AND ALMOND RIBBON SANDWICHES

200g packaged cream cheese, softened
½ teaspoon ground ginger
½ teaspoon five spice powder
180g butter
¼ cup chopped fresh parsley
10 slices wholemeal bread
5 slices white bread
5 slices premium chicken loaf
⅓ cup flaked almonds, toasted

Beat cheese and spices in small bowl with electric mixer until smooth. Beat butter and parsley in bowl until smooth.

Spread 5 slices of wholemeal bread with cheese mixture, top with white bread slices. Spread with half the butter mixture, top with chicken, sprinkle with almonds. Spread remaining wholemeal bread with remaining butter mixture, place butter side down, on chicken. Cut crusts from sandwiches, cut sandwiches into thirds, cut each third into 3 pieces.

Makes 45.
■ Sandwiches can be made several hours ahead.
■ Storage: Covered, in refrigerator.
■ Freeze: Suitable.

PUMPKIN RICOTTA BALLS

200g pumpkin, chopped
4 green shallots, chopped
125g packet cream cheese
125g ricotta cheese
½ teaspoon ground nutmeg
1 teaspoon chopped fresh dill
1½ cups (135g) packaged breadcrumbs
1 egg, lightly beaten
½ cup cornmeal
oil for deep-frying

Boil, steam or microwave pumpkin until soft; drain. Mash pumpkin in bowl; cool. Blend or process pumpkin, shallots, cheeses, nutmeg, dill and breadcrumbs until mixture forms a smooth ball. Roll 2 level teaspoons of mixture into a ball, dip in egg, then toss in cornmeal. Repeat with remaining mixture, egg and cornmeal. Deep-fry in hot oil until browned, drain on absorbent paper; cool before serving.

Makes about 50.
■ Balls can be made 2 days ahead.
■ Storage: Covered, in refrigerator.
■ Freeze: Not suitable.
■ Microwave: Not suitable.

DUCK AND GINGER TARTLETS

1 tablespoon oil
150g duck breast fillet
¼ cup redcurrant jelly, melted
¼ cup fresh parsley sprigs

PASTRY
1 cup plain flour
60g butter
1 egg yolk
2 teaspoons lemon juice
1 tablespoon water, approximately

FILLING
1 large onion, chopped
1½ teaspoons grated fresh ginger
⅓ cup water
2 tablespoons marmalade

Heat oil in pan, add duck, cook until browned all over and tender; cool. Cut duck into thin strips.

Roll pastry on lightly floured surface until 5mm thick. Cut 7cm rounds from pastry, place into greased 12-hole tart tray, prick all over with fork. Bake in moderate oven for about 15 minutes or until lightly browned; cool.

Spoon filling into pastry cases, top with duck, brush with jelly, top with parsley; cover, refrigerate 1 hour before serving.

Pastry: Sift flour into bowl, rub in butter. Add egg yolk, juice and enough water to mix to a firm dough. Knead dough on lightly floured surface until smooth; cover, refrigerate 30 minutes.

Filling: Combine onion, ginger and water in pan. Bring to boil, simmer, covered, for about 15 minutes or until onion is very soft. Blend or process onion mixture and marmalade until smooth; cool.

Makes 12.

■ Tartlets can be made 3 hours ahead.
■ Storage: Covered, in refrigerator.
■ Freeze: Not suitable.
■ Microwave: Not suitable.

ABOVE LEFT: From left: Chicken and Almond Ribbon Sandwiches, Pumpkin Ricotta Balls.
ABOVE: Duck and Ginger Tartlets.

Above left: Plates from Something Special. Above: Plate from Made in Japan; ducks from Country Form

ROAST BEEF
AND GHERKIN TARTLETS

**1½ sheets ready rolled
  shortcrust pastry
100g sliced roast beef, finely
  shredded
4 small gherkins, finely chopped
1 tablespoon chopped fresh parsley
2 tablespoons chopped fresh chives
2 tablespoons tomato paste
¼ cup mayonnaise
¼ cup fresh parsley sprigs, extra**

Cut 4cm squares from pastry, press into
greased 4cm tart pans, prick all over with
fork. Bake in moderate oven for about
10 minutes or until lightly browned; cool.

   Combine beef, gherkins, herbs, paste
and mayonnaise in bowl.
Just before serving, fill pastry cases with
beef mixture, top with extra parsley.
   Makes about 30.
■ Tartlets can be made 2 hours ahead.
■ Storage: Covered, in refrigerator.
■ Freeze: Unfilled pastry cases suitable.
■ Microwave: Not suitable.

AVOCADO ANCHOVY DIP

**1 avocado, mashed
56g can anchovy fillets, drained,
  finely chopped
1 clove garlic, finely chopped
¼ red pepper, finely chopped
1 small onion, finely chopped
2 tablespoons sour cream
1 teaspoon lemon juice**

Combine all ingredients in bowl; cover,
refrigerate 1 hour. Serve with crackers.
   Makes about 1 cup.
■ Dip can be made 3 hours ahead.
■ Storage: Covered, in refrigerator.
■ Freeze: Not suitable.

*ABOVE: Clockwise from front: Roast Beef
and Gherkin Tartlets, Avocado Anchovy Dip,
Chicken and Coriander Toasts.
RIGHT: Clockwise from left: Roast Beef and
Cucumber Mini Sandwiches, Omelette Rolls
with Trout and Pepper Cheese, Pumpernickel
Cheese Truffles.*

Right: Plates from Something Special

CHICKEN AND CORIANDER
TOASTS

**15 slices white bread
250g chicken thigh fillets, chopped
1 egg
2 teaspoons dry sherry
2 teaspoons light soy sauce
2 teaspoons cornflour
½ teaspoon grated fresh ginger
1 tablespoon coconut cream
1 egg, lightly beaten, extra
¼ cup fresh coriander sprigs
oil for deep-frying**

Cut an 8cm square from each bread slice,
cut each square into 4 triangles. Blend or
process chicken, egg, sherry, sauce,
cornflour, ginger and coconut cream until
smooth. Spread each triangle with
chicken mixture, brush lightly with extra
egg, top with a coriander sprig.
Up to 1 hour before serving, deep-fry
triangles in hot oil until well browned; drain
on absorbent paper; cool.
   Makes 60.
■ Toasts can be prepared 1 day ahead.
■ Storage: Covered, in refrigerator.
■ Freeze: Uncooked toasts suitable.
■ Microwave: Not suitable.

OMELETTE ROLLS WITH TROUT AND PEPPER CHEESE

200g green peppercorn cheese
4 eggs
200g smoked trout, chopped
1 small avocado, mashed
2 teaspoons lemon juice

Freeze cheese until firm enough to grate.

Beat eggs in bowl until combined. Pour quarter of egg mixture into heated well-greased heavy-based crepe pan, cook until set, lift onto plate; cover. Repeat with remaining eggs.

Place quarter of trout along a side of 1 omelette, top with some of the combined avocado and juice, then grated cheese. Repeat with remaining omelettes, trout, avocado mixture and cheese. Carefully roll omelettes, wrap in plastic wrap, refrigerate for 2 hours.

Just before serving, cut each roll into 2cm slices.

Makes about 24.

■ Rolls can be prepared a day ahead.
■ Storage: Covered, in refrigerator.
■ Freeze: Not suitable.
■ Microwave: Not suitable.

PUMPERNICKEL CHEESE TRUFFLES

100g butter
¾ cup finely grated Edam cheese
½ teaspoon paprika
pinch cayenne pepper
dash Tabasco sauce
125g pumpernickel bread

Beat butter, cheese, spices and sauce in small bowl with electric mixer until smooth and creamy; cover, refrigerate mixture for 30 minutes.

Blend or process pumpernickel until coarsely crumbed. Roll level teaspoons of cheese mixture in pumpernickel crumbs; cover, refrigerate 30 minutes or until firm.

Makes about 30.

■ Truffles can be made 3 days ahead.
■ Storage: Covered, in refrigerator.
■ Freeze: Suitable.

ROAST BEEF AND CUCUMBER MINI SANDWICHES

60g packaged cream cheese
1 tablespoon chopped fresh chives
40g butter
1 teaspoon seeded mustard
3 slices wholemeal bread
1 small green cucumber, thinly sliced
3 slices light grain bread
100g sliced rare roast beef
3 slices white bread

Beat cheese and chives in bowl. Beat butter and mustard in separate bowl until smooth. Spread cheese mixture over wholemeal bread slices, top with cucumber. Spread butter mixture over grain bread slices, top with beef.

Stack grain bread slices on wholemeal bread slices; top with white bread slices. Cut off crusts, cut each sandwich in half then each half into 4 fingers.

Makes 24.

■ Can be made 1 hour ahead.
■ Storage: Covered, in refrigerator.
■ Freeze: Not suitable.

CREAMY GARLIC CHEESE DIP

250g packet cream cheese
2 tablespoons sour cream
2 tablespoons thickened cream
2 cloves garlic, crushed
2 tablespoons dry white wine
2 tablespoons chopped fresh parsley
2 tablespoons chopped fresh chives

Beat cheese in bowl with electric mixer until smooth. Add creams, garlic, wine and herbs, beat until combined; cover, refrigerate 1 hour. Serve with a variety of fresh vegetables.

Makes about 2 cups.
■ Dip can be made 2 days ahead.
■ Storage: Covered, in refrigerator.
■ Freeze: Not suitable.

SALAMI AND SUN-DRIED TOMATO WEDGES

250g packet soft cream cheese
2 tablespoons chopped fresh basil
6 sun-dried tomatoes, chopped
10 slices white bread
20 slices salami
10 pitted green olives, halved
10 pitted black olives, halved

Blend or process half the cheese with basil until smooth. Blend or process remaining cheese separately with tomatoes until smooth.

Cut rounds from bread the same size as the salami rounds. Spread a slice of salami with basil mixture, top with a bread round. Spread bread with tomato mixture, top with a slice of salami. Repeat with remaining salami, basil mixture, bread and tomato mixture, making 10 stacks. Cover, refrigerate 30 minutes.

Just before serving, cut stacks into 4 wedges, top each wedge with half an olive, secure with toothpick.

Makes 40.
■ Can be prepared 3 hours ahead.
■ Storage: Covered, in refrigerator.
■ Freeze: Not suitable.

BELOW: From left: Creamy Garlic Cheese Dip, Salami and Sun-Dried Tomato Wedges. RIGHT: Smoked Chicken Brioche.

Below: Plates from Mikasa. Right: China from Villeroy & Boch; glasses from Sasaki

SMOKED CHICKEN BRIOCHE

7g compressed yeast
½ teaspoon castor sugar
¼ cup warm water
2 cups plain flour
1 tablespoon castor sugar, extra
1 tablespoon chopped fresh oregano
2 eggs, lightly beaten
90g butter, softened
1 egg yolk
1 tablespoon milk
1 tablespoon rock salt

FILLING
1½ tablespoons oil
1 small onion, chopped
½ cup sun-dried tomatoes, finely
    chopped
125g smoked chicken, finely chopped

Lightly grease mini muffin pans (1 tablespoon capacity). Combine yeast with sugar in bowl, stir in water, cover, stand for about 10 minutes or until mixture is foamy.

Sift flour and extra sugar into bowl, stir in oregano, then combined eggs and yeast mixture, mix to a firm dough. Turn dough onto lightly floured surface, knead for about 5 minutes or until smooth and elastic. Knead in small pieces of butter until all butter is incorporated; this should take about 5 minutes (mixture will be quite sticky at this stage).

Knead dough further 10 minutes or until smooth and elastic. Place dough in lightly oiled bowl, cover, stand in warm place for about 1 hour or until doubled in size.

Knead dough until smooth, divide evenly into 32 portions. Remove a quarter of the dough from each portion. Flatten larger portions of dough into rounds, place a small amount of filling in centre of each round, pinch dough up around filling so filling is enclosed. Place rounds pinched side down in prepared pans, brush tops lightly with a little of the combined egg yolk and milk.

Roll each remaining quarter of dough into a small ball, place on top of rounds in pans. Using a wooden skewer, push skewer through centre of dough to base of pan, remove skewer. Brush tops with remaining milk mixture, sprinkle with salt. Stand in warm place for about 15 minutes or until doubled in size.

Bake in moderately hot oven for 5 minutes, reduce heat to moderate, bake further 10 minutes or until well browned and cooked through. Stand 2 minutes before cooling on wire racks. Repeat with remaining dough.

Filling: Heat oil in pan, add onion, cook, stirring, until onion is soft. Combine onion, tomatoes and chicken in bowl.

Makes 32.

■ Brioche can be made a day ahead.
■ Storage: Covered, in refrigerator.
■ Freeze: Cooked brioche suitable.
■ Microwave: Not suitable.

MINTED PEA AND WHOLEMEAL PASTRY BOATS

1¼ cups wholemeal plain flour
80g butter
¼ cup sour cream
¼ cup sour cream, extra
fresh mint leaves

FILLING
1 cup (125g) frozen peas, thawed
6 fresh mint leaves
pinch chilli powder
1 green shallot, chopped
¼ cup sour cream
1 egg

Sift flour into bowl, rub in butter. Stir in cream, mix to a firm dough. Knead dough gently on lightly floured surface until smooth; cover, refrigerate 30 minutes.

Roll pastry on lightly floured surface until 2mm thick. Cut oval shapes to fit 8cm long pastry boat tins, press pastry into tins, prick all over with fork. Place tins on oven tray, bake in hot oven for about 6 minutes or until dry to touch. Fill each pastry boat with 1½ level teaspoons of filling, bake further 8 minutes or until filling is set. Remove pastry boats from tins, cool on wire rack.

Just before serving, place extra sour cream in piping bag fitted with a small plain tube, pipe along centres of boats, top with mint.
Filling: Blend or process all ingredients until smooth.

Makes about 40.
- Pastry boats can be made a day ahead. Filling can be made separately a day ahead.
- Storage: Pastry boats, in airtight container. Filling, covered, in refrigerator.
- Freeze: Unfilled pastry boats suitable.
- Microwave: Not suitable.

SARDINE CREAM ON PUMPERNICKEL

250g packet cream cheese
¼ cup thickened cream
1 tablespoon chopped fresh chives
1 tablespoon chopped fresh parsley
1 tablespoon chopped fresh dill
1 teaspoon lemon juice
1 teaspoon horseradish cream
dash Tabasco sauce
120g can sardines, drained, mashed
250g packet pumpernickel slices
1½ tablespoons red lumpfish caviar
fresh dill sprigs

Beat cream cheese in small bowl with electric mixer until smooth. Add cream, herbs, juice, horseradish, Tabasco and sardines, beat until smooth. Cover, refrigerate 2 hours or until firm. Cut pumpernickel into 5cm x 3cm rectangles.
Just before serving, spoon mixture into piping bag fitted with fluted tube, pipe onto pumpernickel, top with caviar and dill.

Makes about 40.
- Cream can be made a day ahead.
- Storage: Covered, in refrigerator.
- Freeze: Not suitable.

ABOVE: From left: Sardine Cream on Pumpernickel, Minted Pea and Wholemeal Pastry Boats.
RIGHT: From left: Duck and Orange Pate Crusties, Artichoke Cheese Berets, Tuna Cheese Creams.

Above: Plates from Made in Japan. Right: China from Villeroy & Boch

ARTICHOKE CHEESE BERETS

3 x 400g cans artichoke bottoms,
    drained
1 small red pepper
60g packaged cream cheese
¼ teaspoon drained capers, finely
    chopped
1 gherkin, finely chopped
2 teaspoons mayonnaise
1 hard-boiled egg, finely chopped

Cut a small slice from base of each
artichoke; reserve slices. Cut half the pepper into small sticks; chop remaining pepper finely. Beat cheese in bowl until
smooth. Stir in capers, gherkin, mayonnaise, egg and chopped pepper. Fill
artichokes with cheese mixture. Make a
small cut in reserved artichoke slices,
push in pepper sticks. Place slices on
artichokes, beret style.
    Makes about 24.
■ Recipe can be made 3 hours ahead.
■ Storage: Covered, in refrigerator.
■ Freeze: Not suitable.

TUNA CHEESE CREAMS

125g packet cream cheese
½ cup grated tasty cheese
¼ cup grated fresh parmesan cheese
1 tablespoon sour cream
425g can tuna, drained
1 tablespoon chopped fresh chives
½ teaspoon seeded mustard
2 cups (160g) flaked almonds, toasted

Blend or process cheeses, cream and
tuna until smooth, stir in chives and mustard. Lightly crush almonds. Toss 2 level
teaspoons of cheese mixture into nuts,
press nuts on gently, shape into a ball.
Repeat with remaining mixture and nuts;
cover, refrigerate 1 hour before serving.
    Makes about 55.
■ Recipe can be made a day ahead.
■ Storage: Covered, in refrigerator.
■ Freeze: Not suitable.

DUCK AND ORANGE
PATE CRUSTIES

250g unsalted butter
400g duck and orange pate, chopped
1 teaspoon grated orange rind
1 tablespoon canned drained green
    peppercorns, crushed
⅓ cup chopped fresh chives
2 small French bread sticks

Beat butter in bowl with electric mixer until
smooth. Gradually beat in pate, beat until
smooth. Stir in rind, peppercorns and
chives; mix well.
    Cut each bread stick in half crossways.
Using the end of a wooden spoon, scoop
out bread to form a 1cm shell. Spoon pate
into piping bag fitted with plain tube, pipe
mixture into centres of bread sticks. Wrap
bread tightly in foil, refrigerate several
hours or overnight.
Just before serving, cut bread sticks
evenly into slices.
    Makes about 55.
■ Rounds can be prepared a day ahead.
■ Storage: Covered, in refrigerator.
■ Freeze: Suitable.

FRESH BEETROOT WITH SOUR CREAM IN WITLOF LEAVES

You will need about 5 small witlof.

2 medium (200g) uncooked beetroot, peeled, grated
2 tablespoons orange juice
¼ cup oil
1 tablespoon chopped fresh chives
1 orange
⅓ cup sour cream
50 witlof leaves
fresh chives, extra

Combine beetroot, juice, oil and chives in bowl. Thinly peel rind from orange, cut rind into fine strips. Add strips to pan of simmering water, simmer 5 minutes, drain.

Just before serving, spoon sour cream and beetroot mixture into witlof leaves, top with rind and extra chives.

Makes 50.

- Beetroot and rind can be prepared 3 hours ahead.
- Storage: Covered, in refrigerator.
- Freeze: Not suitable.
- Microwave: Rind suitable.

SMOKED SALMON, CAPER AND DILL TRIANGLES

200g packaged cream cheese
2 teaspoons lemon juice
1 tablespoon fresh dill sprigs
¼ teaspoon drained capers
12 slices white bread
180g sliced smoked salmon

Blend or process cheese, juice, dill and capers until well combined. Spread 1 slice of bread with cheese mixture, top with a layer of salmon.

Spread a second slice of bread with cheese mixture, place cheese side down on salmon. Spread top with cheese mixture, top with a layer of salmon.

Spread a third slice of bread with cheese mixture, place cheese side down on salmon. Trim crusts from sandwich, cut into 8 triangles. Repeat with remaining bread, cheese mixture and salmon.

Makes 32.

- Triangles can be made 2 hours ahead.
- Storage: Covered, in refrigerator.
- Freeze: Not suitable

CURRIED CHICKEN AND TOMATO TARTLETS

25 slices white bread
30g butter, melted
1 tablespoon oil
fresh coriander leaves

FILLING
2 tablespoons oil
1 onion, chopped
2 teaspoons curry powder
1 teaspoon apricot jam
2 tablespoons dry red wine
1 bay leaf
2 tablespoons water
½ cup mayonnaise
½ cup cooked chopped chicken
1 tomato, seeded, chopped
1 tablespoon chopped fresh coriander

Lightly grease 12-hole tart trays. Cut 2 x 5cm rounds from each slice of bread, roll rounds with rolling pin until thin. Place rounds into prepared trays, brush lightly with combined butter and oil. Place another tart tray on top of bread, press down, bake in moderate oven for 8 minutes. Remove top tray, bake further 2 minutes or until bread cases are lightly browned; cool. Repeat with remaining bread rounds.

Just before serving, spoon filling into bread cases, top with coriander leaves.

Filling: Heat oil in pan, add onion and curry powder, cook, stirring, until onion is soft. Stir in jam, wine, bay leaf and water. Bring to boil, simmer, uncovered, for about 10 minutes or until liquid is reduced by about three-quarters, strain, reserve the liquid; cool. Combine reserved liquid, mayonnaise, chicken, tomato and coriander in bowl.

Makes 50.

- Cases can be made 2 days ahead. Filling can be made 3 hours ahead.
- Storage: Cases, in airtight container. Filling, covered, in refrigerator.
- Freeze: Not suitable.
- Microwave: Not suitable.

RIGHT: Clockwise from front: Fresh Beetroot with Sour Cream in Witlof Leaves, Smoked Salmon, Caper and Dill Triangles, Curried Chicken and Tomato Tartlets.
China from Villeroy & Boch

AVOCADO PISTACHIO PATE WITH HERB TOASTS

1½ cups mashed avocado
125g packet cream cheese
2 green shallots, chopped
1 small clove garlic, crushed
1 teaspoon lemon juice
¼ teaspoon chilli powder
2 tablespoons chopped
   pistachio nuts
1 teaspoon chopped fresh parsley

HERB TOASTS
2 Lebanese bread rounds
40g butter, melted
½ teaspoon dried rosemary leaves
½ teaspoon dried basil leaves
½ teaspoon dried thyme leaves

Blend or process avocado, cheese, shallots, garlic, juice and chilli until smooth. Line 2 moulds (1 cup capacity) with plastic wrap, sprinkle nuts into base of each mould, pour in avocado mixture. Cover, refrigerate 3 hours or until set.

Just before serving, unmould pate, remove plastic, sprinkle lightly with parsley. Serve pate with herb toasts.

Herb Toasts: Split bread rounds horizontally. Brush each half with butter; sprinkle with combined herbs. Place on oven trays, bake in moderate oven for about 10 minutes or until lightly browned; cool. Break rounds into pieces.

   Makes about 2 cups pate.

■ Both can be made a day ahead.
■ Storage: Herb toasts, in airtight container. Pate, covered, in refrigerator.
■ Freeze: Not suitable.
■ Microwave: Not suitable.

PIMIENTO, CORN AND BACON SPIRALS

130g can creamed corn
1 tablespoon chopped fresh parsley
¾ cup stale breadcrumbs
3 bacon rashers, finely chopped
1 clove garlic, crushed
5 green shallots, chopped
200g can pimientos, drained, chopped
⅓ cup grated fresh parmesan cheese
8 sheets fillo pastry
30g butter, melted
2 tablespoons oil

Combine corn, parsley and ¼ cup of the breadcrumbs in bowl; mix well. Cook bacon in pan until crisp, add garlic and shallots, cook, stirring, until shallots are soft, drain on absorbent paper.

Combine bacon mixture with half the remaining breadcrumbs in bowl. Combine pimientos, cheese and remaining breadcrumbs in another bowl.

Layer 4 pastry sheets together, brushing each with some of the combined butter and oil. Starting at a long edge and leaving 4cm border along opposite edge, spread half the corn mixture lengthways over one-third of pastry. Cover centre third with half the bacon mixture, then sprinkle half the pimiento mixture over remaining third.

Tightly roll up pastry from the corn side, brush lightly with butter mixture. Place roll on tray, cover, refrigerate 1 hour.

Repeat with remaining pastry, butter mixture, corn mixture, bacon mixture and pimiento mixture. Cut rolls into 1cm slices, place slices on greased oven trays, bake in moderately hot oven for about 15 minutes or until well browned. Cool spirals on trays.

Makes about 50.
■ Rolls can be made a day ahead.
■ Storage: Covered, in refrigerator.
■ Freeze: Uncooked rolls suitable.
■ Microwave: Not suitable.

FAR LEFT: Avocado Pistachio Pate with Herb Toasts.
ABOVE: Pimiento, Corn and Bacon Spirals.

Far left: Plates from Mikasa. Above: China from Mikasa

MINI CHICKEN DRUMSTICKS

12 (about 1kg) chicken wings
MARINADE
¼ teaspoon five spice powder
¼ teaspoon turmeric
⅔ cup dry red wine
2 tablespoons oil
1 bay leaf
1 tablespoon barbecue sauce

Cut first joint from wings. Separate second and third joints. Holding small end of third joint, trim around bone with sharp knife. Cut, scrape and push meat down to large end. Using fingers, pull skin and meat over end of bone. Repeat with second joints, carefully removing 1 bone from each joint.

Combine drumsticks and marinade in bowl; mix well. Cover, refrigerate several hours or overnight.

Drain drumsticks, place on wire rack, place rack on oven tray. Bake in moderate oven for about 10 minutes or until chicken is tender; cool. Wrap exposed ends of bone in foil, refrigerate until cold.
Marinade: Combine all ingredients in bowl; mix well.

Makes 24.
■ Drumsticks can be made a day ahead.
■ Storage: Covered, in refrigerator.
■ Freeze: Suitable.
■ Microwave: Suitable.

TOMATOES WITH CREAMY SMOKED OYSTER FILLING

2 x 250g punnets cherry tomatoes
105g can smoked oysters, drained
100g packaged cream cheese
2 tablespoons lemon juice
fresh mustard cress

Slice tops from tomatoes, scoop out seeds, drain tomatoes upside down on absorbent paper for 30 minutes. Blend or process oysters, cheese and juice; cover, refrigerate 30 minutes.

Spoon oyster mixture into piping bag fitted with fluted tube, pipe mixture into tomatoes, top with mustard cress.

Makes about 40.
■ Recipe can be made 3 hours ahead.
■ Storage: Covered, in refrigerator.
■ Freeze: Not suitable.

QUICK HERB TOASTIES

100g butter
1 clove garlic, crushed
2 tablespoons chopped fresh parsley
1 tablespoon chopped fresh basil
1 tablespoon chopped fresh chives
1 teaspoon chopped fresh thyme
10 slices white bread

Beat butter, garlic and herbs in small bowl with electric mixer until creamy and combined. Cut crusts from bread, spread both sides of bread with herb butter, cut bread diagonally into quarters. Place quarters on ungreased oven tray, bake in moderate oven for about 20 minutes or until lightly toasted; cool.

Makes 40.
■ Toasties can be made a day ahead.
■ Storage: In airtight container.
■ Freeze: Uncooked toasties suitable.
■ Microwave: Not suitable.

RIGHT: Clockwise from front: Quick Herb Toasties, Mini Chicken Drumsticks, Tomatoes with Creamy Smoked Oyster Filling.

China from Villeroy & Boch

GRAVLAX ON MINI BUCKWHEAT BLINIS

It is correct that the salmon is not cooked in this recipe.

250g fillet Atlantic salmon
⅓ cup sugar
¼ cup coarse cooking salt
2 teaspoons ground black pepper
⅓ cup chopped fresh dill
⅓ cup chopped fresh chives
2 tablespoons finely chopped
   avocado
2 teaspoons lemon juice
fresh dill sprigs, extra

BLINIS
¾ cup buckwheat flour
2 teaspoons sugar
1 egg, lightly beaten
½ cup milk
30g butter, melted
½ teaspoon cream of tartar
¼ teaspoon bicarbonate of soda
1 tablespoon water

HERB BUTTER
60g butter
1 teaspoon chopped fresh dill
1 teaspoon chopped fresh chives

Remove skin and bones from salmon. Combine sugar, salt, pepper and herbs in bowl. Sprinkle half the sugar mixture on tray covered with plastic wrap. Place salmon on top of sugar mixture, sprinkle remaining sugar mixture over top of salmon. Cover tightly with plastic wrap; refrigerate overnight.

Rinse salmon quickly and gently under cold water, pat dry with absorbent paper. Slice salmon thinly.

Just before serving, combine avocado and juice in bowl. Spread blinis evenly with herb butter, top with salmon slices, avocado and extra dill sprigs.

Blinis: Combine flour and sugar in bowl, gradually stir in combined egg, milk and butter, stir until smooth; cover, stand 1 hour. Stir in combined cream of tartar, soda and water.

Cook 4 blinis at a time. For each blini, spoon 2 level teaspoons of mixture into heated greased heavy-based pan, turn blinis when bubbles appear, cook until browned underneath. Cool on wire racks.

Herb Butter: Combine all ingredients in bowl; mix well.

Makes about 25.

■ Gravlax and herb butter can be made 2 days ahead. Blinis can be made 6 hours ahead.
■ Storage: Gravlax and herb butter, covered, in refrigerator. Blinis, in air-tight container.
■ Freeze: Blinis suitable.
■ Microwave: Not suitable.

CHICKEN CHEESE BALLS

1 cup (150g) chopped cooked chicken
125g packet cream cheese
1½ teaspoons French mustard
2 tablespoons lemon juice
1 cup (125g) salted mixed nuts

Blend or process chicken, cheese, mustard and juice until smooth; cover, refrigerate 1 hour.

Blend or process nuts until fine. Roll 2 level teaspoons of chicken mixture into a ball, toss in nuts.

Repeat with remaining mixture and nuts; cover, refrigerate for 1 hour.

Makes about 30.

■ Balls can be made a day ahead.
■ Storage: Covered, in refrigerator.
■ Freeze: Not suitable.

PUMPKIN AND FETA ROUNDS

250g pumpkin
1 medium (125g) potato
8 slices white bread
60g ghee, melted
50g feta cheese, chopped
2 teaspoons chopped fresh chives

HERB BUTTER
45g butter
1 tablespoon chopped fresh chives
1 tablespoon chopped fresh parsley

Boil, steam or microwave pumpkin and potato until tender, drain well. Mash pumpkin and potato in bowl, push through sieve; cover, refrigerate until cold.

Cut 6 x 3½cm rounds from each slice of bread. Combine ghee and bread rounds in bowl, stir until well coated, place rounds on oven tray. Bake in moderate oven for about 15 minutes or until lightly browned; cool.

Just before serving, thinly spread rounds with herb butter. Spoon pumpkin mixture into piping bag fitted with fluted tube. Pipe mixture onto rounds, top with cheese and chives.

Herb Butter: Combine butter, chives and parsley in bowl; mix well.

Makes 48.

■ Rounds can be made a week ahead. Butter can be made 2 days ahead.
■ Storage: Rounds, in airtight container. Butter, covered, in refrigerator.
■ Freeze: Rounds and butter suitable.
■ Microwave: Vegetables suitable.

LEFT: Gravlax on Mini Buckwheat Blinis.
BELOW: From front: Pumpkin and Feta Rounds, Chicken Cheese Balls.

Left: China from Villeroy & Boch. Below: Plates, tray and glasses from The Country Trader

CREAMY ASPARAGUS MOUSSE

440g can green asparagus spears
60g butter
4 green shallots, chopped
1 tablespoon plain flour
½ cup cream
2 teaspoons French mustard
dash Tabasco sauce
½ cup grated tasty cheese
1½ tablespoons gelatine
¼ cup water

Lightly oil 22cm ring mould. Drain asparagus, reserve liquid. Blend or process asparagus until smooth. Heat butter in pan, add shallots, cook, stirring, until soft. Stir in flour, cook until bubbling. Remove from heat, gradually stir in combined asparagus, reserved liquid, cream, mustard and sauce. Stir over heat until sauce boils and thickens.

Remove from heat, add cheese, stir until smooth, push mixture through sieve.

Sprinkle gelatine over water in cup, stand in small pan of simmering water, stir until dissolved; cool slightly.

Stir gelatine into asparagus mixture; pour into prepared mould; cover, refrigerate until set. Serve mousse with melba toast, if desired.

■ Mousse can be made a day ahead.
■ Storage: Covered, in refrigerator.
■ Freeze: Not suitable.
■ Microwave: Suitable.

QUAIL WITH PEPPERCORN AND PORT SAUCE

12 quail breasts, skinned
30g butter
1 teaspoon oil

PEPPERCORN AND PORT SAUCE
2 green shallots, chopped
¼ cup redcurrant jelly
2 teaspoons lemon juice
2 teaspoons port
1 teaspoon canned drained green
peppercorns, crushed

Cut quail breasts in half. Heat butter and oil in pan, add quail, cook on both sides until lightly browned and tender, drain on absorbent paper; cool. Serve cold quail with peppercorn sauce.

Peppercorn and Port Sauce: Drop shallots into small pan of boiling water; remove from heat, stand 1 minute; drain. Combine shallots, jelly, juice, port and peppercorns in pan, stir over heat until jelly is melted; cool to room temperature.

Makes 24.
■ Can be prepared 3 hours ahead.
■ Storage: Covered, in refrigerator.
■ Freeze: Uncooked quail suitable.
■ Microwave: Sauce suitable.

PARSLEY ANCHOVY DIP WITH CROUTONS

½ small onion, finely chopped
2 teaspoons drained capers, chopped
2 anchovy fillets, chopped
½ cup chopped fresh
flat-leafed parsley
1 tablespoon lemon juice
¼ cup olive oil
6 pitted black olives, chopped

CROUTONS
2 small French bread sticks, thinly
sliced
60g butter, melted
1 tablespoon oil

Combine all ingredients in bowl; mix well, cover, refrigerate several hours. Serve dip with croutons.

Croutons: Brush bread with combined butter and oil, place on oven tray, bake in moderate oven for about 5 minutes or until crisp; cool.

Makes about 1 cup dip.
■ Dip can be made a day ahead.
Croutons can be made 2 days ahead.
■ Storage: Dip, covered, in refrigerator.
Croutons, in airtight container.
■ Freeze: Croutons suitable.
■ Microwave: Not suitable.

ABOVE: From left: Quail with Peppercorn and Port Sauce, Creamy Asparagus Mousse.
ABOVE RIGHT: From front: Parsley Anchovy Dip with Croutons, Red Pepper Toasts.

RED PEPPER TOASTS

2 large (500g) red peppers
1 tablespoon olive oil
2 tablespoons brown sugar
⅓ cup dry white wine
2½ tablespoons balsamic vinegar
2 tablespoons chopped fresh basil
⅓ loaf unsliced white bread
½ lime, thinly sliced

Cut peppers in quarters, remove membrane and seeds. Grill peppers, skin side up, until skin blackens and blisters; peel skins from peppers. Finely chop peppers. Heat oil in pan, stir in peppers and sugar, cook over low heat, covered, for about 45 minutes or until peppers are soft, stirring occasionally. Stir wine and vinegar into pan, bring to boil, simmer, uncovered, for about 15 minutes or until thick, remove from heat; strain, cool, stir in basil.

Cut bread into 5mm slices, cut 2½cm squares from slices, place squares on ungreased oven tray. Bake in moderate oven for about 10 minutes or until lightly browned; cool. Spoon pepper mixture onto toast squares, top with lime wedges. Makes about 80.

■ Peppers can be prepared a day ahead; toasts made 2 days ahead.
■ Storage: Peppers, covered, in refrigerator. Toast, in airtight container.
■ Freeze: Toast squares suitable.
■ Microwave: Not suitable.

BRANDIED CHEESES ON PUMPERNICKEL

125g pepper cheese
125g neufchatel cheese
2 teaspoons brandy
pinch paprika
⅓ cup thickened cream
1 bacon rasher, chopped
250g packet pumpernickel slices
4 dried apricot halves, sliced
2 teaspoons chopped fresh chives

Blend or process cheeses, brandy and paprika until smooth. Transfer mixture to bowl. Whip cream in small bowl until soft peaks form, fold into cheese mixture; cover, refrigerate 30 minutes.

Cook bacon in pan until crisp, drain on absorbent paper; cool. Cut pumpernickel into 1½cm x 4cm fingers.

Just before serving, spoon cheese mixture into piping bag fitted with fluted tube. Pipe mixture onto pumpernickel, top with bacon, apricots and chives.

Makes about 48.
- Cheese mixture can be prepared a day ahead.
- Storage: Covered, in refrigerator.
- Freeze: Not suitable.
- Microwave: Bacon suitable.

PIQUANT FISH AND LETTUCE PARCELS

We used mullet fillets in this recipe. It is correct that the fish is not cooked in this recipe, but appears and tastes cooked due to the marinating.

500g fish fillets
¼ cup white vinegar
½ cup lemon juice
1 teaspoon salt
1 tablespoon chopped fresh dill
10 butter lettuce leaves

Skin fillets, chop fish into 2cm cubes. Combine fish, vinegar, juice, salt and dill; cover, refrigerate several hours or overnight. Cut lettuce into 2cm strips.

Just before serving, drain fish, wrap in lettuce, secure with toothpicks.

Makes about 36.
- Recipe can be prepared a day ahead.
- Storage: Covered, in refrigerator.
- Freeze: Not suitable.

CREAM CHEESE OLIVES IN SALAMI

50g packaged cream cheese
3 green shallots, finely chopped
¼ teaspoon paprika
40 (350g) large pimiento-stuffed green olives
400g sliced salami

Blend or process cheese, shallots and paprika until smooth. Spoon mixture into piping bag fitted with small plain tube, pipe mixture into olives, pushing pimiento to end of each olive. Fold salami slices in half, secure around olive with toothpicks.

Makes 40.
- Recipe can be made 3 hours ahead.
- Storage: Covered, in refrigerator.
- Freeze: Not suitable.

RIGHT: Clockwise from front: Cream Cheese Olives in Salami, Brandied Cheeses on Pumpernickel, Piquant Fish and Lettuce Parcels.

HERBED CHEESE AND SMOKED SALMON TARTLETS

1²⁄₃ cups plain flour
125g butter
2 eggs, lightly beaten
150g smoked salmon slices
¼ cup fresh dill leaves

HERBED CHEESE
500g neufchatel cheese
1½ tablespoons lemon juice
1 tablespoon chopped fresh chives
2 tablespoons chopped fresh dill

Lightly grease 12-hole mini muffin pans (1 tablespoon capacity). Sift flour into bowl, rub in butter, add eggs, mix to a firm dough. Knead dough gently on lightly floured surface until smooth; cover, refrigerate 30 minutes.

Roll dough on floured surface until 2mm thick. Cut 5½cm rounds from dough, place into prepared pans, prick all over with fork. Bake in moderately hot oven for about 10 minutes or until browned; cool in pans. Cut salmon into 5cm strips.

Just before serving, fill pastry cases with herbed cheese, top with salmon strips and dill leaves.

Herbed Cheese: Beat cheese and juice in bowl with electric mixer until smooth. Stir in herbs; mix well.

Makes about 55.

- Pastry cases and herbed cheese can be prepared separately 2 days ahead.
- Storage: Pastry cases, in airtight container. Herbed cheese, covered, in refrigerator.
- Freeze: Unfilled pastry cases suitable.
- Microwave: Not suitable.

CURRIED YOGURT LAMB TARTLETS

1 sheet ready rolled shortcrust pastry
2 teaspoons chopped fresh mint

FILLING
200g lamb fillet
1 tablespoon oil
¼ small red pepper, finely chopped
¼ cup plain yogurt
1 teaspoon curry powder
2 teaspoons chopped fresh mint

Cut 4½cm rounds from pastry, press into greased 4cm round fluted tart pans, place pans on oven tray, bake in moderate oven for about 10 minutes or until lightly browned; cool.

Just before serving, spoon filling into tartlet cases, sprinkle with mint.

Filling: Trim excess fat from lamb. Heat oil in pan, add lamb, cook until browned all over and tender; cool. Cut lamb into fine strips; combine with pepper, yogurt, curry powder and mint in bowl.

Makes about 25.
- Tartlet cases can be made a week ahead; filling made a day ahead.
- Storage: Tartlet cases in airtight container. Filling, covered, in refrigerator.
- Freeze: Unfilled tartlet cases suitable.
- Microwave: Not suitable.

BRANDIED BLUE CHEESE AND DATES ON CRACKERS

150g mild blue vein cheese
100g packaged cream cheese
1 teaspoon brandy
1 teaspoon chopped fresh chives
4 fresh dates, pitted
25 water crackers
fresh parsley sprigs

Beat cheeses, brandy and chives in small bowl with electric mixer until combined. Cut dates into thin strips.

Just before serving, spoon cheese mixture into piping bag fitted with fluted tube, pipe onto crackers, top with date strips and parsley.

Makes about 25.
- Cheese mixture can be prepared 2 days ahead.
- Storage: Cover, in refrigerator.
- Freeze: Not suitable.

LEFT: Herbed Cheese and Smoked Salmon Tartlets.
ABOVE: From left: Brandied Blue Cheese and Dates on Crackers, Curried Yogurt Lamb Tartlets.

Above: China from Villeroy & Boch

LAMB ROLLS WITH ROSEMARY HOLLANDAISE

2 large (about 400g) lamb fillets
1½ tablespoons lemon juice
1 tablespoon oil
¼ teaspoon dried rosemary leaves
4 green shallots

ROSEMARY HOLLANDAISE
1 tablespoon water
2 teaspoons lemon juice
¼ teaspoon dried rosemary leaves
6 black peppercorns
1 egg yolk
60g butter, chopped

Trim excess fat from lamb. Combine juice, oil and rosemary in dish, add lamb, mix well; cover, refrigerate overnight.

Heat baking dish, add lamb, cook over high heat until browned all over, bake in moderate oven for about 15 minutes or until tender; cool.

Cut green tops from shallots, cut tops into thin strips. Cut lamb crossways into 2mm slices (if lamb fillets are very thin, cut slices thicker and flatten with rolling pin). Spread each slice with rosemary hollandaise, roll up slices. Tie each roll with a shallot strip.

Rosemary Hollandaise: Combine water, juice, rosemary and peppercorns in pan, bring to boil, simmer, uncovered, until liquid is reduced to 3 teaspoons, strain; reserve liquid. Whisk egg yolk and reserved liquid in top half of double saucepan or in heatproof bowl, whisk over simmering water until mixture begins to thicken. Remove from heat, whisk in butter gradually, whisk between additions.

Makes about 50.
- Rolls can be made 6 hours ahead.
- Storage: Covered, in refrigerator.
- Freeze: Not suitable.
- Microwave: Not suitable.

HERBED TOMATO LOBSTER

1½ cup tomato juice
1 teaspoon chopped fresh chives
1 teaspoon chopped fresh basil
250g uncooked lobster tail
20g butter
1 teaspoon oil
1 tablespoon lime juice
5 slices white bread
30g butter, melted, extra

Combine tomato juice, chives and basil in bowl. Cut shell from underside of lobster. Remove flesh from shell, cut flesh into 2cm cubes.

Heat butter, oil and lime juice in pan, add lobster, cook, stirring, until just tender. Combine lobster with tomato mixture while hot; cover, refrigerate 3 hours.

Cut 4 x 3½cm rounds from bread, brush both sides of rounds with extra butter. Place rounds on oven trays, bake in moderate oven for 10 minutes, turn rounds, bake further 10 minutes or until lightly browned; cool.

Just before serving, drain lobster, serve on toast rounds.
Makes 20.
- Lobster and toast rounds can be prepared separately a day ahead.
- Storage: Lobster, covered, in refrigerator. Toast rounds, in airtight container.
- Freeze: Not suitable.
- Microwave: Not suitable.

PROSCIUTTO EGG ROLLS

12 quail eggs
¼ teaspoon grated lime rind
40g packaged cream cheese
2 tablespoons finely grated smoked cheese
1 teaspoon chopped fresh basil
6 slices (60g) prosciutto

Place eggs in pan, cover with cold water, bring to boil, simmer, uncovered, for 3 minutes. Drain eggs; rinse under cold water; cool, remove shells.

Combine rind, cheeses and basil in bowl. Cut eggs in half. Cut prosciutto in half lengthways, cut into 7cm strips. Spread cheese mixture onto each strip, wrap a prosciutto strip around egg.
Makes 24.
- Recipe can be made 6 hours ahead.
- Storage: Covered, in refrigerator.
- Freeze: Filling suitable.
- Microwave: Not suitable.

GINGER BEEF KEBABS

½ teaspoon wasabi
2 teaspoons light soy sauce
¼ cup mashed avocado
¼ teaspoon lemon juice
20g butter, softened
¼ cup glace ginger
10 slices rare roast beef

Blend or process wasabi, sauce, avocado, juice and butter until smooth; cover, refrigerate 30 minutes.

Cut ginger into 1cm pieces. Spread beef slices with avocado mixture, cut into 1½cm x 12cm strips. Place a piece of ginger on centre of each beef strip, fold strips in half, thread onto toothpicks. Cover, refrigerate 1 hour before serving.
Makes about 30.
- Recipe can be made 3 hours ahead.
- Storage: Covered, in refrigerator.
- Freeze: Not suitable.

LEFT: From front: Lamb Rolls with Rosemary Hollandaise, Herbed Tomato Lobster, Prosciutto Egg Rolls.
BELOW: Ginger Beef Kebabs.

MINCED LAMB KEBABS WITH GARLIC MINT YOGURT

500g minced lamb
1 onion, grated
1 teaspoon ground cumin
1 teaspoon ground coriander
2 tablespoons chopped fresh parsley
2 tablespoons oil

GARLIC MINT YOGURT
1 cup plain yogurt
2 tablespoons chopped fresh mint
1 clove garlic, crushed

Process mince, onion, cumin, coriander and parsley until smooth. Shape 2 level teaspoons of mixture into a ball. Repeat with remaining mixture. Thread balls onto skewers; cover, refrigerate several hours or overnight.

Heat oil in pan, add kebabs, cook until browned all over and cooked through; drain on absorbent paper. Cover, refrigerate several hours or until required. Serve kebabs with garlic mint yogurt.
Garlic Mint Yogurt: Combine all ingredients in bowl; mix well.

Makes about 25.
■ Recipe can be made a day ahead.
■ Storage: Covered, in refrigerator.
■ Freeze: Kebabs suitable.
■ Microwave: Not suitable.

CHICKEN TARRAGON PATE

500g chicken livers
¼ cup port
125g butter
6 green shallots, chopped
1 clove garlic, crushed
1 tablespoon chopped fresh tarragon
½ cup thickened cream
2 tablespoons brandy
125g butter, extra

Combine livers and port in bowl; cover, refrigerate 2 hours.

Heat half the butter in pan, add shallots and garlic, cook, stirring, until shallots are soft. Add liver mixture, cook, stirring, until livers are lightly browned. Stir in tarragon, remove from heat.

Melt remaining butter in separate pan. Blend or process liver mixture until smooth. While motor is operating, gradually add butter, cream and brandy, process until smooth. Strain mixture into serving dishes; cover, refrigerate until firm.

Heat extra butter in pan until bubbling, stand 10 minutes; pour clear butter over pate. Cover, refrigerate until set. Serve pate with melba toast, if desired.

Makes about 2 cups.
■ Pate can be made 3 days ahead.
■ Storage: Covered, in refrigerator.
■ Freeze: Not suitable.
■ Microwave: Not suitable.

CHICKEN LIVER PATE

50g butter
1 small onion, chopped
2 cloves garlic, chopped
250g chicken livers
1½ tablespoons port
1 teaspoon canned drained
   green peppercorns
1 tablespoon chopped fresh basil
¼ cup cream
12 slices wholemeal bread, toasted

Heat butter in pan, add onion and garlic, cook, stirring, until onion is soft. Add livers, cook, stirring, until livers change colour. Stir in port, peppercorns, basil and cream. Blend or process mixture until smooth, transfer to bowl; cover, refrigerate several hours or until firm.

Cut 4 x 4cm rounds from each slice of toast. Beat pate with electric mixer until smooth, spoon into piping bag fitted with fluted tube, pipe pate onto toasts, garnish with fresh herbs, if desired.

Makes 48.
■ Pate can be made 2 days ahead.
   Toasts can be made 6 hours ahead.
■ Storage: Pate, covered, in refrigerator.
   Toasts, in airtight container.
■ Freeze: Not suitable.
■ Microwave: Not suitable.

CAMEMBERT PASTRAMI SQUARES

125g camembert
30g butter
1 teaspoon mayonnaise
2 teaspoons chopped fresh chives
250g packet pumpernickel squares
6 slices (100g) pastrami
2 tablespoons chopped fresh
**   chives, extra**

Remove rind from camembert, stand camembert at room temperature until soft.

Beat butter, camembert and mayonnaise in small bowl with electric mixer until smooth, stir in chives. Spread each pumpernickel square with a level teaspoon of camembert mixture.

Cut pastrami into 2cm squares, roll up, place onto squares, top with remaining cheese mixture and extra chives.

Makes about 20.
- Recipe can be made 2 hours ahead.
- Storage: Covered, in refrigerator.
- Freeze: Not suitable.

SPINACH AND PIMIENTO CREPE ROLLETTES

¾ cup plain flour
3 eggs, lightly beaten
1 tablespoon oil
⅔ cup milk
250g packet frozen spinach, thawed

FILLING
⅔ cup sour cream
2 x 200g cans pimientos,
**   drained, chopped**
2 tablespoons chopped fresh chives

Sift flour into bowl, gradually stir in eggs, oil and milk, beat until smooth. Squeeze excess moisture from spinach, stir spinach into batter.

Pour 2 to 3 tablespoons of batter into heated greased heavy-based crepe pan, cook until lightly browned underneath, turn crepe, cook until lightly browned underneath. Roll crepe while hot; cool. Repeat with remaining batter.

Unroll crepes, spread evenly with filling, roll up. Cut rolls into 2cm slices; cover, refrigerate for 1 hour before serving.

Filling: Combine all ingredients in bowl. Makes about 55.
- Recipe can be made a day ahead.
- Storage: Covered, in refrigerator.
- Freeze: Unfilled crepes suitable.
- Microwave: Not suitable.

LEFT: From left: Minced Lamb Kebabs with Garlic Mint Yogurt, Chicken Tarragon Pate. ABOVE: Clockwise from top: Camembert Pastrami Squares, Chicken Liver Pate, Spinach and Pimiento Crepe Rollettes.

Sift flour into bowl, stir in cheese. Rub in butter, press mixture firmly together into a ball (or process all ingredients to form a ball). Cover, refrigerate 30 minutes.

Roll pastry between sheets of greaseproof paper until 3mm thick. Cut 2½cm rounds from pastry, place onto lightly greased oven trays, sprinkle half the rounds with paprika. Bake in moderately hot oven for about 8 minutes or until lightly browned; cool on trays. Sandwich plain and paprika topped crisps with filling.

Filling: Stand cheese in bowl at room temperature for 30 minutes. Beat in cream and basil, beat until smooth.

Makes about 45.

- Crisps and filling can be made separately 2 days ahead.
- Storage: Crisps, in airtight container. Filling, covered, in refrigerator.
- Freeze: Unfilled crisps suitable.
- Microwave: Not suitable.

MINI LETTUCE ROLLS WITH MINTY YOGURT SAUCE

1 iceberg lettuce
20g butter
1 small red pepper, chopped
75g baby mushrooms, chopped
1 small zucchini, grated
1 small carrot, grated
2 green shallots, chopped
2 tablespoons grated
   parmesan cheese

MINTY YOGURT SAUCE
1 cup plain yogurt
2 tablespoons chopped fresh mint
½ teaspoon castor sugar

Separate lettuce leaves, trim thick stalks from leaves. Drop leaves into pan of boiling water, drain immediately. Plunge into bowl of iced water, drain; pat dry with absorbent paper.

Heat butter in pan, add pepper, mushrooms, zucchini, carrot and shallots, cook, stirring, until pepper is soft. Stir in cheese; cool to room temperature.

Cut lettuce leaves into 8cm x 12cm rectangles, top each rectangle with a level tablespoon of pepper mixture, fold in sides, roll up firmly. Serve rolls with sauce.

Minty Yogurt Sauce: Combine all ingredients in bowl.

Makes about 20.

- Lettuce rolls can be made 1 hour ahead. Sauce, made a day ahead.
- Storage: Covered, in refrigerator.
- Freeze: Not suitable.
- Microwave: Not suitable.

CORIANDER LAMB CROQUETTES

2 teaspoons grated fresh ginger
500g lamb mince
2 cloves garlic, crushed
1 onion, grated
1 tablespoon light soy sauce
2 tablespoons chopped fresh
   coriander
1 medium carrot, grated
1 egg, lightly beaten
1 cup stale breadcrumbs
packaged breadcrumbs
oil for deep-frying

SAUCE
½ cup plum sauce
½ teaspoon light soy sauce
2 teaspoons chopped fresh coriander

Press ginger between 2 spoons to extract juice; discard pulp. Combine juice, mince, garlic, onion, sauce, coriander, carrot, egg and stale breadcrumbs in bowl. Toss level tablespoons of mixture into packaged breadcrumbs, shape into croquettes, place on tray; cover, refrigerate 30 minutes. Deep-fry croquettes in hot oil until well browned and cooked through, drain on absorbent paper; cool. Cover, refrigerate until cold. Serve croquettes with sauce.

Sauce: Combine all ingredients in bowl. Makes about 35.

- Recipe can be made a day ahead.
- Storage: Covered, in refrigerator.
- Freeze: Uncooked croquettes suitable.
- Microwave: Not suitable.

CHEESE CRISPS

½ cup self-raising flour
½ cup grated fresh parmesan cheese
60g butter
2 teaspoons paprika

FILLING
½ cup grated havarti cheese
1½ tablespoons cream
2 teaspoons chopped fresh basil

ABOVE LEFT: From back: Coriander Lamb Croquettes, Cheese Crisps.
ABOVE RIGHT: Clockwise from left: Cheese and Bacon Dip with Caraway Crackers, Bocconcini and Prosciutto with Mustard Mayonnaise, Mini Lettuce Rolls with Minty Yogurt Sauce.

BOCCONCINI AND PROSCIUTTO WITH MUSTARD MAYONNAISE

100g prosciutto
200g bocconcini, chopped

MUSTARD MAYONNAISE
½ cup mayonnaise
2 teaspoons seeded mustard
2 teaspoons chopped fresh basil

Cut prosciutto into 1½cm x 6cm strips, wrap around bocconcini pieces, press ends of prosciutto firmly. Serve bites with mustard mayonnaise.
Mustard Mayonnaise: Combine mayonnaise, mustard and basil in bowl; mix well.
　Makes about 35.
■ Bites and mayonnaise can be made 6 hours ahead.
■ Storage: Covered, in refrigerator.
■ Freeze: Not suitable.

CHEESE AND BACON DIP WITH CARAWAY CRACKERS

4 bacon rashers, thinly sliced
500g ricotta cheese
⅓ cup sour cream
1 tablespoon chopped fresh chives
1 teaspoon seeded mustard
⅓ cup flaked almonds, toasted

CARAWAY CRACKERS
250g packet Jatz crackers
½ cup grated tasty cheese
½ cup grated fresh parmesan cheese
¼ teaspoon chilli powder
1 teaspoon caraway seeds

Cook bacon in pan until crisp and well browned, drain on absorbent paper; cool.
　Blend or process ricotta cheese and sour cream until smooth. Stir in bacon, chives, mustard and almonds. Serve dip with caraway crackers.

Caraway Crackers: Place crackers on oven trays in single layer, sprinkle evenly with combined cheeses, chilli and seeds. Bake in moderate oven for about 10 minutes or until cheese is melted; cool.
　Makes about 2 cups dip.
■ Dip and crackers can be made several hours ahead.
■ Storage: Dip, covered, in refrigerator. Crackers, in airtight container.
■ Freeze: Not suitable.
■ Microwave: Not suitable.

SMOKED TURKEY QUICHES

4 sheets fillo pastry
60g butter, melted
2 tablespoons cranberry sauce
4 slices (about 75g) smoked turkey
   breast roll, sliced
¼ cup grated tasty cheese
⅓ cup milk
⅓ cup cream
1 egg, lightly beaten
1 tablespoon chopped fresh chives

Lightly grease mini muffin pans (1 tablespoon capacity). Layer pastry sheets together, brushing each sheet lightly with butter. Cut 5½cm rounds from pastry, ease into prepared pans. Bake in moderate oven for about 5 minutes or until lightly browned. If pastry cases are puffed, flatten centres slightly while warm; cool.

Divide cranberry sauce, turkey and cheese between cases. Combine remaining ingredients in jug, pour into cases. Bake in moderate oven for about 15 minutes or until set; cool.

Makes about 30.
■ Pastry cases can be made 2 days
   ahead. Quiches can be cooked
   2 hours ahead.
■ Storage: Covered, in refrigerator.
■ Freeze: Not suitable.
■ Microwave: Not suitable.

BABY MUSHROOMS WITH CREAMY EGG

30 (about 300g) baby mushrooms
3 hard-boiled eggs
1 tablespoon sour cream
1 tablespoon mayonnaise
2 teaspoons chopped fresh chives
1 tablespoon chopped fresh parsley
¼ teaspoon ground black pepper
¼ teaspoon French mustard

Remove stems from mushrooms; keep stems for another use. Mash eggs with remaining ingredients in bowl.
Just before serving, spoon egg mixture into mushrooms.
   Makes 30.
■ Egg filling can be made a day ahead.
   Mushrooms, filled 1 hour ahead.
■ Storage: Covered, in refrigerator.
■ Freeze: Not suitable.

SESAME BEEF ON CUCUMBER

500g piece rump steak
¼ cup dark soy sauce
1 clove garlic, crushed
1 tablespoon sesame seeds
1 teaspoon sesame oil
1 tablespoon oil
1 long green cucumber
¼ small red pepper

Trim excess fat from steak, wrap steak in plastic wrap, freeze 30 minutes.

Cut steak into very thin slices, cut slices into thin strips. Combine strips, sauce, garlic, seeds and sesame oil in shallow glass dish; cover, refrigerate 3 hours.

Heat half the oil in pan, add half the beef, cook for about 2 minutes or until well browned all over; drain, cool. Repeat with remaining oil and beef.

Peel 4 thin strips lengthways from cucumber skin, cut cucumber crossways into 4mm slices. Cut pepper into long thin strips. Top cucumber slices with beef and pepper.

Makes about 30.
■ Recipe can be made 3 hours ahead.
■ Storage: Covered, in refrigerator.
■ Freeze: Not suitable.
■ Microwave: Not suitable.

BELOW: From left: Smoked Turkey Quiches, Baby Mushrooms with Creamy Egg.
RIGHT: Clockwise from front: Sesame Beef on Cucumber, Smoked Eel Pate, Turkey Mignonette Parcels.

Right: Plates from Villa Italiana

TURKEY MIGNONETTE PARCELS

100g roast turkey breast roll, chopped
1 tablespoon mango chutney, chopped
2 tablespoons mayonnaise
1 teaspoon seeded mustard
20 mignonette lettuce leaves

Combine turkey, chutney, mayonnaise and mustard in bowl. Remove thick centres from lettuce leaves. Drop leaves into pan of boiling water, drain immediately, drop into bowl of iced water. Drain leaves, pat dry with absorbent paper.

Place a level teaspoon of turkey mixture on centre of a lettuce leaf, fold up to form a parcel. Repeat with remaining lettuce and turkey mixture.

Makes 20.

■ Filling can be made a day ahead. Parcels can be made an hour ahead.
■ Storage: Covered, in refrigerator.
■ Freeze: Not suitable.
■ Microwave: Not suitable.

SMOKED EEL PATE

400g smoked eel, skinned, boned
½ cup sour cream
3 teaspoons lemon juice
1 tablespoon marsala
50g butter, melted

Blend or process eel, cream, juice and marsala until smooth. Push mixture through sieve to remove fine bones. Stir in butter; cover, refrigerate until firm. Serve with selection of fresh salad vegetables and melba toast, if desired.

Makes about 1 cup.

■ Pate can be made 2 days ahead.
■ Storage: Covered, in refrigerator.
■ Freeze: Suitable.

MARINATED MUSHROOMS

⅔ cup cider vinegar
½ cup oil
1 teaspoon sugar
2 tablespoons chopped fresh parsley
1 clove garlic, crushed
350g (about 35) baby mushrooms, halved

Combine vinegar, oil, sugar, parsley and garlic in bowl; mix well. Add mushrooms, stir to coat; cover, refrigerate several hours or overnight. Drain mushrooms before serving.

Makes about 70.
■ Can be made 2 days ahead.
■ Storage: Covered, in refrigerator.
■ Freeze: Not suitable.

SMOKED EEL AND GHERKIN SQUARES

2 tablespoons mayonnaise
2 teaspoons chopped fresh dill
2 teaspoons chopped fresh coriander
80g packet mini toast
150g smoked eel, skinned, sliced
2 gherkins, sliced
1 teaspoon chopped fresh red chillies

Combine mayonnaise, dill and coriander in bowl; spread thinly over toasts. Arrange eel and gherkins over mayonnaise, sprinkle with a little chilli.

Makes about 30.
■ Squares can be made 2 hours ahead.
■ Storage: Covered, in refrigerator.
■ Freeze: Not suitable.

APRICOT CHICKEN BALLS

375g minced chicken
½ cup packaged breadcrumbs
1 egg
½ cup finely chopped dried apricots
½ cup finely chopped macadamias
1 tablespoon light soy sauce
3 teaspoons chopped fresh coriander
fresh coriander leaves, extra

Blend or process chicken, breadcrumbs, egg, apricots, nuts, sauce and chopped coriander until well combined. Roll 2 level teaspoons of mixture into a ball, top with an extra coriander leaf. Repeat with remaining mixture and extra coriander. Place balls in top half of steamer in single layer, cook, covered, over boiling water for about 8 minutes or until cooked through; cool, refrigerate.

Makes about 50.
■ Balls can be made a day ahead.
■ Storage: Covered, in refrigerator.
■ Freeze: Uncooked balls suitable.
■ Microwave: Not suitable.

RIGHT: Clockwise from back: Apricot Chicken Balls, Smoked Eel and Gherkin Squares, Marinated Mushrooms.

BEEF WALDORF TARTS

1 sheet ready rolled shortcrust pastry
2 tablespoons chopped red pepper

FILLING
100g sliced rare roast beef, chopped
1/4 cup finely chopped apple
1/2 teaspoon lemon juice
2 tablespoons finely chopped celery
**1 1/2 tablespoons finely chopped
   walnuts or pecans**
1 tablespoon chopped gherkin
2 tablespoons sour cream
2 teaspoons mayonnaise

Lightly grease 12-hole tart trays. Cut 4 1/2cm rounds from pastry, ease pastry into prepared trays, cover with rounds of greaseproof paper, fill with dried beans or rice. Bake in moderate oven for about 7 minutes, remove paper and beans, bake further 5 minutes or until lightly browned; cool.

Just before serving, spoon filling into pastry cases, top with pepper.
Filling: Combine beef, apple, juice, celery, nuts, gherkin, cream and mayonnaise in bowl; mix well.
    Makes about 25.
■ Pastry cases can be made 2 days ahead. Filling, made 2 hours ahead.
■ Storage: Pastry cases, in airtight container. Filling, covered in refrigerator.
■ Freeze: Unfilled pastry cases suitable.
■ Microwave: Not suitable.

CHICKEN AND PRUNE PINWHEELS

2/3 cup (150g) pitted prunes
4 large chicken breast fillets
1 litre (4 cups) water
**2 large chicken stock cubes,
   crumbled**

Soak prunes in boiling water for about 15 minutes or until softened. Drain prunes, blend or process until smooth. Pound chicken between sheets of greaseproof paper until thin. Spread chicken with prune mixture, roll up chicken from narrow ends, wrap rolls tightly in foil.

Combine water and stock cubes in pan, bring to boil, add rolls to water. Simmer, covered, for about 15 minutes or until chicken is cooked. Drain rolls; cool, refrigerate until cold.
Just before serving, unwrap rolls, cut into 1 1/2cm slices.
    Makes about 20.
■ Can be made 2 days ahead.
■ Storage: Covered, in refrigerator.
■ Freeze: Uncooked rolls suitable.
■ Microwave: Not suitable.

SALMON AND SPINACH PINWHEELS

8 English spinach leaves,
  roughly chopped
1 egg
½ cup drained flaked salmon
2 green shallots
¼ cup plain flour
½ cup milk
75g packaged cream cheese,
  softened
1½ tablespoons red lumpfish caviar

Steam spinach until tender, drain, squeeze excess moisture from spinach. Blend or process spinach, egg, salmon and shallots until combined. With motor operating, gradually add flour and milk, process until smooth.

Pour 2 to 3 tablespoons of batter into heated greased heavy-based crepe pan; cook until lightly browned underneath. Turn crepe, brown on other side. Repeat with remaining batter; cool. Spread crepes with a thin layer of cream cheese, then caviar. Roll crepes tightly; cover, refrigerate for 1 hour.

Just before serving, cut crepe rolls into 1½cm slices.

Makes about 30.
- Pinwheels can be made a day ahead.
- Storage: Covered, in refrigerator.
- Freeze: Not suitable.
- Microwave: Not suitable.

NUTTY CHICKEN RIBBON SANDWICHES

15 slices grain bread
90g butter, softened
1½ cups (200g) finely chopped
  cooked chicken
1 stick celery, finely chopped
1½ tablespoons sour cream
2 tablespoons mayonnaise
⅓ cup chopped pistachios

Spread 1 side of each bread slice with butter. Combine chicken, celery, sour cream, mayonnaise and nuts in bowl; mix well. Spread 5 slices of bread with half the chicken mixture, top with buttered bread, buttered side down. Spread with remaining chicken mixture, top with buttered bread, buttered side down.

Cut crusts from sandwiches, cut sandwiches into thirds, cut each third into 2 pieces.

Makes 30.
- Can be made 3 hours ahead.
- Storage: Covered, in refrigerator.
- Freeze: Suitable.

LEFT: From left: Beef Waldorf Tarts, Chicken and Prune Pinwheels.
BELOW: From front: Nutty Chicken Ribbon Sandwiches, Salmon and Spinach Pinwheels.

Left: China from Wedgwood. Below: Platter from Villa Italiana

CORN AND PIMIENTO FRITTERS WITH HERBED TUNA

130g can corn kernels, drained
1/3 cup chopped drained
    canned pimientos
3 eggs, lightly beaten
1 teaspoon lemon pepper
2/3 cup plain flour
fresh thyme sprigs

TOPPING
2 (about 300g) tuna steaks
1/4 teaspoon dried chilli flakes
2 teaspoons chopped fresh coriander
2 teaspoons chopped fresh basil
1 teaspoon chopped fresh thyme
1 teaspoon grated lime rind
1 tablespoon lime juice
1 tablespoon oil
1/4 teaspoon sugar

HERB CREAM
1/2 cup sour cream
1 teaspoon chopped fresh basil
1 teaspoon chopped fresh chives
1/2 teaspoon chopped fresh thyme
1 teaspoon lime juice

Combine corn, pimientos, eggs and pepper in bowl, stir in sifted flour, mix well. Using 2 level teaspoons of mixture per fritter, spoon mixture into hot greased pan, cook until lightly browned underneath. Turn fritters, brown other side; drain on absorbent paper, cool.

Just before serving, top fritters with topping, herb cream and thyme sprigs.

Topping: Place tuna in bowl, combine remaining ingredients in separate bowl, pour over tuna; cover, refrigerate 1 hour. Add undrained tuna mixture to heated pan, cook for about 5 minutes each side or until cooked through; cool. Cut tuna into thin slices.

Herb Cream: Combine sour cream, herbs and juice in bowl.

Makes about 30.

- Fritters and topping can be made a day ahead. Herb cream can be made 3 days ahead.
- Storage: Covered, in refrigerator.
- Freeze: Not suitable.
- Microwave: Not suitable.

WHOLEMEAL PIKELETS WITH CREAMY EGG TOPPING

1 cup wholemeal self-raising flour
1 egg, lightly beaten
1 cup milk
2 teaspoons seeded mustard
20g butter, melted
30g salmon roe

TOPPING
4 hard-boiled eggs, halved
2 tablespoons mayonnaise
2 tablespoons sour cream
2 tablespoons chopped fresh chives

Sift flour into bowl, gradually stir in combined egg and milk; beat to a smooth batter. Stir in mustard and butter.

Drop teaspoons of mixture into heated greased heavy-based pan. Turn pikelets when bubbles appear, brown on other side; cool.

Just before serving, spread topping onto pikelets, top with roe. Sprinkle with extra chives, if desired.

Topping: Remove yolks from eggs, mash yolks in bowl. Finely chop egg whites, stir into yolks with mayonnaise, sour cream and chives; mix well.

Makes about 90.

- Can be prepared 6 hours ahead.
- Storage: Pikelets, in airtight container. Topping, covered, in refrigerator.
- Freeze: Pikelets suitable.
- Microwave: Not suitable.

PIMIENTO PROSCIUTTO EGGS

6 hard-boiled eggs, halved
1 tablespoon mayonnaise
1 tablespoon thickened cream
1 tablespoon chopped drained canned pimiento
1 tablespoon chopped fresh basil
3 slices (about 30g) prosciutto, finely chopped
1 tablespoon chopped fresh basil, extra
1 tablespoon chopped drained canned pimiento, extra

Remove yolks from eggs, mash yolks in bowl with mayonnaise and cream. Stir in pimiento, basil and prosciutto. Spoon mixture into egg whites, top with extra basil and extra pimiento.

Makes 12.

- Eggs can be made 3 hours ahead.
- Storage: Covered, in refrigerator.
- Freeze: Not suitable.

SUN-DRIED TOMATOES WITH CABANOSSI AND CHEESE

30cm piece cabanossi
14 sun-dried tomato halves, drained
200g matured provolone cheese, chopped
1/3 cup fresh basil leaves

Slice cabanossi diagonally into 7mm slices. Cut each tomato half into thirds. Thread cabanossi, tomato, cheese and basil onto cocktail skewers.

Makes 42.

- Kebabs can be made 3 hours ahead.
- Storage: Covered, in refrigerator.
- Freeze: Not suitable.

LEFT: Corn and Pimiento Fritters with Herbed Tuna.
ABOVE: Clockwise from back: Pimiento Prosciutto Eggs, Sun-Dried Tomatoes with Cabanossi and Cheese, Wholemeal Pikelets with Creamy Egg Topping.

BRIE, EGG AND SMOKED TROUT TRIANGLES

2 eggs, lightly beaten
40g butter, softened
2 teaspoons grated lime rind
6 slices white bread
100g sliced smoked trout
125g brie
6 slices rye bread
¼ cup sour cream

Pour half the egg into heated greased 20cm omelette pan, cook until just set. Remove omelette from pan, cool. Repeat with remaining egg.

Beat butter and rind in bowl until combined. Spread white bread slices with butter mixture, top with trout. Remove rind from brie, beat brie in bowl until smooth, spread evenly over trout. Cut omelettes to fit bread, place on brie. Spread rye bread with cream, place, cream side down, onto omelette layer; press lightly.

Cut crusts from sandwiches. Cut sandwiches into 8 triangles.

Makes 48.

■ Can be made 4 hours ahead.
■ Storage: Covered, in refrigerator.
■ Freeze: Not suitable.

ABOVE: Brie, Egg and Smoked Trout Triangles.
ABOVE RIGHT: Clockwise from back: Bacon Crackers with Parsley Dip, Olives in Cheese Pastry, Mini Minted Lamb Pikelets.

Above: Serving ware from Private Life. Above right: Plates from Villa Italiana

BACON CRACKERS WITH PARSLEY DIP

5 bacon rashers, chopped
⅔ cup self-raising flour
¼ cup wholemeal plain flour
½ cup grated fresh parmesan cheese
¼ cup cornmeal
½ teaspoon caraway seeds
50g butter
⅓ cup plain yogurt
2 tablespoons French mustard

PARSLEY DIP
1 cup chopped fresh parsley
¼ cup chopped fresh mint
1 clove garlic, crushed
1 small red pepper, finely chopped
1 small onion, finely chopped
¼ cup olive oil
2 tablespoons lemon juice
½ teaspoon ground black pepper

Cook bacon in pan until crisp; drain on absorbent paper; cool. Blend or process bacon, flours, cheese, cornmeal and seeds until bacon is finely chopped. Add butter, process until well combined; transfer mixture to bowl. Stir in combined yogurt and mustard, mix to a soft dough. Knead dough on lightly floured surface until smooth; cover, refrigerate dough 30 minutes.

Roll dough on lightly floured surface until 2mm thick. Cut into 5½cm rounds, place rounds onto lightly greased oven trays. Bake in moderate oven for about 15 minutes or until browned; cool.

Parsley Dip: Combine all ingredients in bowl; cover, refrigerate for 4 hours.

Makes about 50 crackers.
Makes about 1½ cups dip.

■ Crackers can be made a week ahead. Dip can be made a day ahead.
■ Storage: Crackers, in airtight container. Dip, covered, refrigerated.
■ Freeze: Not suitable.
■ Microwave: Not suitable.

MINI MINTED LAMB PIKELETS

⅓ cup self-raising flour
2 tablespoons wholemeal self-raising flour
¼ teaspoon bicarbonate of soda
1 egg, lightly beaten
⅓ cup milk
½ teaspoon white vinegar
2 teaspoons butter, melted
2 teaspoons chopped fresh mint

MINT BUTTER
60g butter, softened
2 tablespoons mint jelly

MINTED LAMB
20g butter
1 clove garlic, crushed
200g lamb fillets
1 tablespoon mint jelly

Sift dry ingredients into bowl, gradually st in combined egg, milk and vinegar, beat t a smooth batter; stir in butter (or blend process these ingredients until smooth).

Drop level teaspoons of batter int heated greased heavy-based pan. Coo until bubbles appear, turn pikelets, brow other side; cool.

Just before serving, spread mint butter over pikelets, top with minted lamb, sprinkle with mint.

Mint Butter: Beat butter and jelly in bowl until combined.

Minted Lamb: Heat butter and garlic in pan, add lamb, cook until well browned all over and tender; cool. Cut lamb into thin strips, return to pan with jelly, stir over heat until combined; cool.

Makes about 40.

■ Recipe can be prepared a day ahead.
■ Storage: Pikelets, in airtight container. Mint butter and minted lamb, covered, in refrigerator.
■ Freeze: Pikelets suitable.
■ Microwave: Not suitable.

OLIVES IN CHEESE PASTRY

1 cup plain flour
pinch cayenne pepper
100g butter
1¼ cups (150g) grated tasty cheese
50 small stuffed green olives
1 egg, lightly beaten
poppy seeds

Process flour, pepper and butter until combined. Add cheese, process until mixture forms a ball. Knead dough on lightly floured surface until smooth; cover, refrigerate 30 minutes. Drain olives on absorbent paper.

Roll pastry between sheets of greaseproof paper until 3mm thick. Cut 4cm rounds from pastry, top each round with an olive, fold pastry around olives to enclose, roll into balls.

Dip tops of balls in egg, then seeds. Place balls onto greased oven tray; cover, refrigerate 30 minutes.

Bake in moderately hot oven for about 15 minutes or until browned; cool.

Makes 50.

■ Recipe can be made a day ahead.
■ Storage: In airtight container.
■ Freeze: Not suitable.
■ Microwave: Not suitable.

LEMON GRASS AND CHILLI BEEF PARCELS

2 teaspoons butter
400g beef fillet, chopped
2 tablespoons finely chopped fresh
   lemon grass
2 small fresh red chillies, finely
   chopped
4 green shallots, chopped
2 tablespoons tomato paste
¼ cup water
12 large cabbage leaves

Heat butter in pan, add beef, cook, stirring, until well browned. Stir in lemon grass, chillies and shallots, cook, stirring, until shallots are soft. Stir in paste and water; cool to room temperature.

Trim thick stalks from cabbage leaves; cut leaves in half. Steam leaves until wilted, drain on absorbent paper. Spoon beef mixture onto narrow end of each leaf half, fold sides in, roll up, secure with toothpicks. Cover, refrigerate until cold.
   Makes 24.
■ Parcels can be made 6 hours ahead.
■ Storage: Covered, in refrigerator.
■ Freeze: Not suitable.
■ Microwave: Cabbage suitable.

LAMB IN CUCUMBER CUPS

4 green cucumbers
1 tablespoon oil
6 green shallots, finely chopped
½ stick celery, finely chopped
1 small fresh green chilli,
   finely chopped
500g minced lamb
1 small clove garlic, crushed
½ teaspoon grated fresh ginger
1 tablespoon dark soy sauce
½ teaspoon honey
2 teaspoons cornflour
1 tablespoon water
1 tablespoon chopped fresh coriander

Cut cucumbers into 1½cm slices. Carefully scoop out some seeds from each slice to form a cup. Heat oil in pan, add shallots, celery and chilli, cook, stirring, until celery is soft.

Add lamb, garlic and ginger, cook, stirring, until lamb is browned. Stir in blended sauce, honey, cornflour and water, stir until mixture boils and thickens slightly; cool. Spoon lamb mixture into cucumber cups, sprinkle with coriander.
   Makes about 50.
■ Cups can be made 6 hours ahead.
■ Storage: Covered, in refrigerator.
■ Freeze: Not suitable.
■ Microwave: Not suitable.

CHICKEN AND BEETROOT FILLO NESTS

3 sheets fillo pastry
30g butter, melted
1 cup (150g) finely chopped
   cooked chicken
¼ cup sour cream
½ teaspoon garam masala
fresh coriander leaves

BEETROOT RELISH
1 small (125g) uncooked beetroot
1 small onion, finely chopped
1 tablespoon castor sugar
¼ teaspoon grated lemon rind
1 teaspoon lemon juice
¼ cup white vinegar
¼ teaspoon coriander seeds
¼ teaspoon cumin seeds
1 clove garlic, crushed
pinch chilli powder

Lightly grease mini muffin pans (1 tablespoon capacity). Layer pastry sheets together, brushing each sheet lightly with butter; cut into 6cm squares.

Gently press squares into prepared pans. Bake in moderately hot oven for about 5 minutes or until well browned. Cool in pan 5 minutes before turning onto wire rack to cool.

Combine chicken, cream and garam masala in bowl. Spoon a level teaspoon of mixture into each pastry case.
Just before serving, spoon beetroot relish into nests, top with coriander leaves.
Beetroot Relish: Cut beetroot into 3mm slices, cut into 2cm strips. Combine beetroot, onion, sugar, rind, juice, vinegar, seeds, garlic and chilli in pan. Bring to boil, simmer, uncovered, for about 20 minutes or until most of the liquid is evaporated.
   Makes about 30.
■ Pastry cases can be made a day
   ahead. Relish can be made
   2 weeks ahead.
■ Storage: Pastry cases, in airtight container. Relish, covered, in refrigerator.
■ Freeze: Not suitable.
■ Microwave: Relish suitable.

ABOVE LEFT: Chicken and Beetroot Fillo Nests.
RIGHT: Clockwise from back: Crab Mousse, Lamb in Cucumber Cups, Lemon Grass and Chilli Beef Parcels.

CRAB MOUSSE

2 (about 500g) cooked blue
   swimmer crabs
1 small red pepper
½ cup sour cream
2 tablespoons lemon juice
1 tablespoon chopped fresh chives
2 teaspoons gelatine
1 tablespoon water

Lightly oil 2 moulds (¾ cup capacity). Remove flesh from body and claws of crab; you will need 180g crab meat.

Cut pepper into quarters, remove seeds and membrane, place pepper skin side up on oven tray, grill until skin blackens and blisters; cool. Remove skin from pepper, chop pepper roughly.

Blend or process pepper, sour cream, juice and chives until smooth. Sprinkle gelatine over water in cup, stand in small pan of simmering water, stir until gelatine is dissolved; cool. Fold crab and gelatine into pepper mixture, pour into prepared moulds; cover, refrigerate until set.

Just before serving, unmould mousse onto plates, serve with crackers if desired.

Makes about 1½ cups.

■ Mousse can be made a day ahead.
■ Storage: Covered, in refrigerator.
■ Freeze: Not suitable.
■ Microwave: Gelatine suitable.

Glossary

Here are some terms, names and alternatives to help everyone understand and use our recipes perfectly.

ALCOHOL: is optional but adds special flavour; use juice or water to make up the liquid content in a recipe.

ALMONDS, FLAKED: sliced almonds.

BACON RASHERS: bacon slices.

BAKING PAPER: non-stick parchment paper used for lining cake pans and oven trays.

BAKING POWDER: a raising agent consisting of an alkali and an acid. It is mostly made from cream of tartar and bicarbonate of soda in the proportion of 1 level teaspoon of cream of tartar to ½ level teaspoon bicarbonate of soda. This is equivalent to 2 level teaspoons baking powder.

BAMBOO SKEWERS: can be used instead of metal skewers if soaked in water overnight or for several hours to prevent burning during cooking. They are available in several different lengths.

BARBECUE SAUCE: a spicy sauce available from most supermarkets.

BEEF:

EYE FILLET: tenderloin.

MINCED BEEF: ground beef.

SCOTCH FILLET: cut from the rib area.

BEETROOT: regular round beet.

BICARBONATE OF SODA: also known as baking soda.

BOCCONCINI: small balls of mild, delicate cheese packaged in water or whey to keep them white and soft. The water should be just milky and cheese should be white; yellowing indicates that it is too old.

BOK CHOY (Chinese chard): discard stems, use leaves and young tender parts of stems. It requires only a short cooking time such as stir-frying.

BREADCRUMBS:

PACKAGED: use commercially packaged breadcrumbs.

STALE: use 1 or 2-day-old bread; crumbed by grating, blending or processing.

BUTTER: we used sweet (salted) or unsalted butter in our recipes; 125g butter is equal to 1 stick butter.

BUTTERMILK: the liquid left from cream after separation; slightly sour in taste. Substitute skim milk, if preferred.

CABANOSSI: a type of sausage; also known as cabana.

CARDAMOM: an expensive spice with an exotic fragrance. It can be bought in pod, seed or ground form.

CHEESE:

CREAM: also known as Philly.

FETA: a fresh, soft Greek cheese with a slightly crumbly texture and a sharp, salty flavour.

GRUYERE: a Swiss cheese with small holes and a nutty, slightly salty flavour.

HAVARTI: a semi-soft Danish cheese.

JARLSBERG: a Norwegian cheese made from cows' milk; it has large holes and a mild nutty taste.

NEUFCHATEL: soft unripened or fresh curd cheese. It resembles cream cheese but contains more moisture.

PARMESAN: sharp-tasting cheese used as a flavour accent.

PEPPER: a semi-soft cheese containing green peppercorns.

PEPPERED CAMEMBERT: a fresh camembert cheese containing green peppercorns with herbs in the rind.

PROCESSED CHEDDAR: we used a processed cheese which has 22 percent fat content.

PROVOLONE: we used an aged provolone with a firm grainy texture and pronounced spicy flavour.

RICOTTA: we used cheese with 10 percent fat content.

SOFT CREAM CHEESE: also known as Soft Philly, do not substitute for cream cheese in our recipes.

SWISS: we used a mild Swiss style cheese such as St Claire.

TASTY: use a firm good-tasting cheddar.

CHESTNUTS: we used canned whole chestnuts (marrons).

CHICKEN:

CHICKEN LOAF: processed pressed luncheon style loaf.

DOUBLE BREAST FILLETS: filleted chicken breasts still joined in centre.

PREMIUM: we used a large sliced chicken loaf available at delicatessens.

CHILLIES: are available in many different types and sizes. The small ones (bird's eye or bird peppers) are the hottest. Use tight rubber gloves when chopping fresh chillies as they can burn your skin.

CHILLI POWDER: ground dried chillies.

CHIPOLATA SAUSAGES: small cocktail sausages in various flavours.

COCONUT CREAM: available in cans and cartons in supermarkets and Asian stores; canned coconut milk can be substituted, although it is not as thick.

CORIANDER: also known as cilantro and Chinese parsley, is essential to many South-East Asian cuisines; its seeds are the main ingredient of curry powder. A strongly flavoured herb, use it sparingly until you are accustomed to the unique flavour. Parsley can be used instead but tastes quite different. Coriander is available fresh, ground and in seed form.

CORN, CREAMED: available in various sized cans from most supermarkets.

CORNFLOUR: cornstarch.

CORNMEAL: polenta.

CRAB, BLUE SWIMMER: any fresh crab can be substituted.

CRANBERRY SAUCE: cranberries preserved in sugar syrup; has an astringent flavour.

CREAM:

THICKENED (WHIPPING) CREAM: is specified when necessary in recipes.

CREAM: is simply a light pouring cream, also known as half 'n' half.

SOUR CREAM: a thick commercially cultured soured cream.

CRUNCHY OAT BRAN CEREAL: a low-fat, high-fibre toasted breakfast cereal based on oat bran.

CRUSHED NUTS: crushed peanuts.

CUCUMBER: we used large green cucumbers (telegraph cucumbers) and small green cucumbers (Lebanese cucumbers) in this book.

CUMIN: available in seed or ground form; it is another component of commercial curry powder.

EGG NOODLES: we used fine fresh egg noodles in this book. They are available from Asian food stores.

EGG PASTRY SHEETS: we used 10cm

squares in packets available from Asian food stores.

FENNEL SEEDS: fennel seeds are a component of curry powder.
FISH FILLETS, WHITE: we used flake; any white fish can be used.
FISH SAUCE: an essential ingredient in the cooking of a number of South-East Asian countries, including Thailand and Vietnam. It is made from the liquid drained from salted, fermented anchovies. It has a very strong aroma and taste. Use sparingly until you acquire the taste.
FIVE SPICE POWDER: a pungent mixture of spices which includes cinnamon, cloves, fennel, star anise and Szechwan peppers.
FLOUR:
BESAN: is made from ground chick peas; also known as gram or chick pea flour.
BUCKWHEAT: flour milled from buckwheat.
WHITE PLAIN: all-purpose flour.
WHITE SELF-RAISING: substitute plain (all-purpose) flour and baking powder in the proportion of ¾ metric cup plain flour to 2 level metric teaspoons of baking powder. Sift together several times before using. If using 8oz measuring cup, use 1 level cup plain flour to 2 level teaspoons baking powder.
WHOLEMEAL: wholewheat flour without the addition of baking powder.
WHOLEMEAL SELF-RAISING (wholewheat): add baking powder as above to make wholemeal self-raising flour.
FRENCH BREAD STICK: long, thin, crisp white bread stick.

GARAM MASALA: there are many variations of the combinations of cardamom, cinnamon, cloves, coriander, cumin and nutmeg used to make up this spice used often in Indian cooking. Sometimes pepper is used to make a hot variation. It is readily available in jars.
GHEE: clarified butter.
GHERKIN: cornichon.
GINGER:
FRESH, GREEN OR ROOT: scrape away skin and grate, chop or slice ginger as required. Fresh, peeled ginger can be preserved with enough dry sherry to cover; keep in jar in refrigerator; it will keep for months.
GLACE: fresh ginger root preserved in sugar syrup; crystallised ginger can be substituted; rinse off the sugar with warm water, dry ginger well before using.
GROUND: should not be substituted for fresh ginger in any recipe.
PICKLED: is dyed and preserved in rice wine and sugar; we used the pink variety.

GRAND MARNIER: an orange-flavoured liqueur. Cointreau can be substituted.
GREEN GINGER WINE: an Australian-made alcoholic sweet wine infused with fresh ginger.

HERBS: we have specified when to use fresh or dried herbs. We used dried (not ground) herbs in the proportion of 1:4 for fresh herbs, eg, 1 teaspoon dried herbs instead of 4 teaspoons (1 tablespoon) chopped fresh herbs.
HOISIN SAUCE: a thick sweet Chinese barbecue sauce made from salted black beans, onions and garlic.
HORSERADISH CREAM: paste of horseradish, oil, mustard and flavourings.

JAM: conserve.
JATZ BISCUITS: savoury salty crackers.

KUMARA: an orange sweet potato.

LAMB:
FILLET: a very small tender cut found between the loin and chump.
RIBLETS: rib ends closest to the breast, also called spareribs.
LARD: Fat obtained from melting down and clarifying pork fat; available packaged.
LEMON GRASS: available from Asian food stores and needs to be bruised or chopped before using. It will keep in a jug of water at room temperature for several weeks; the water must be changed daily. It can be bought dried; to reconstitute, place several pieces of dried lemon grass in a bowl; cover with hot water, stand 20 minutes; drain. This amount is a substitute for 1 stem of fresh lemon grass.
LEMON PEPPER SEASONING: is a blend of crushed black pepper, salt, lemon, herbs and spices.
LEMON SPREAD: lemon curd or lemon cheese.
LETTUCE: we used iceberg lettuce unless otherwise stated.
LOBSTER: crayfish.
LUMPFISH CAVIAR: this is not a true caviar, but an economical substitute; red and black varieties are available.

MARSALA: a sweet fortified wine.
MILK: we used full cream milk.
MINT JELLY: contains sugar, food acids, pectin, mint etc.
MIRIN: a sweet rice wine used in Japanese cooking. Substitute 1 teaspoon sugar and 1 teaspoon dry sherry for each tablespoon mirin.
MULLET: an oily, strong-flavoured

variety of deep sea fish.
MUSTARD:
DRY: in powdered form.
SEEDED: a French style of mustard with crushed mustard seeds.

NUTRI-GRAIN: breakfast cereal made from corn, oats and wheat.

OIL: polyunsaturated vegetable oil.
OLIVE: virgin oil is obtained only from the pulp of high-grade fruit. Pure olive oil is pressed from the pulp and kernels of second grade olives.
OYSTER CASES: small vol-au-vent cases made from puff or flaky pastry, available in 60g and 75g packets.
OYSTER SAUCE: a rich brown sauce made from oysters cooked in salt and soy sauce, then thickened with starches.

PARSLEY (flat-leafed): also known as Italian or continental parsley.
PASTRAMI: highly seasoned smoked beef ready to eat when bought.
PEPITAS: pumpkin seed kernels.
PEPPERS (capsicums): we used red and green bell peppers in this book.
PIMIENTOS: red peppers (capsicums) canned or bottled in brine or vinegar; sometimes called sweet red pimientos or sweet red peppers.
PLUM SAUCE: a dipping sauce which consists of plums preserved in vinegar, sweetened with sugar and flavoured with chillies and spices.
POLENTA: known as cornmeal or maizemeal; ground from Indian corn.
PORK, BARBECUED: roasted pork fillets available from many Asian fresh food and specialty stores.
POTATOES: we used old potatoes unless otherwise specified.
SWEET: we used the white variety.
PRAWNS (shrimp): most of the recipes in this book use uncooked (green) prawns; they must be shelled and deveined before use.
PROSCIUTTO: uncooked, unsmoked ham cured in salt; it is ready to eat when purchased.
PRUNES: dried plums.
PUFF PASTRY: available frozen from super-markets in blocks and ready-rolled sheets.

RICE PAPER: edible paper available from Asian food stores and gourmet food shops.
RIND: zest.
ROCKMELON: cantaloupe.

SALMON, ATLANTIC: farmed variety of fish available all year.

SAMBAL OELEK (uelek or ulek): a paste made from ground chillies and salt.

SEAFOOD STICKS: made from Alaskan pollack flavoured with crab.

SESAME OIL: made from roasted, crushed white sesame seeds. Use in small quantities. Do not use for frying.

SHALLOTS, GREEN: also known as scallions and spring onions. Do not confuse with small golden shallots.

SOYA CRISPS: savoury snacks made from extruded soy beans.

SOY SAUCE: made from fermented soy beans. The light sauce is generally used with white meat for flavour, and the darker variety with red meat for colour. There is a multi-purpose salt-reduced sauce available, also Japanese soy sauce. It is personal taste which sauce you use.

SPINACH (silverbeet): remove coarse white stems, cook green leafy parts as individual recipes indicate.

SPINACH, ENGLISH: a soft-leaved vegetable, more delicate in taste than silverbeet; however, young silverbeet can be substituted.

SPRING ROLL WRAPPERS OR PASTRY: are sold frozen in Asian food stores in several different sizes. Thaw before using, keep covered with a damp cloth until ready to use.

SQUID (calamari): a type of mollusc. Cleaned squid hoods are available.

STOCK CUBES: available in beef, chicken or vegetable. Use 1 large crumbled stock cube to every 2 cups water. Remember that these cubes contain salt.

SUGAR:
BROWN: soft, fine, brown sugar.
CASTOR: fine granulated table sugar.
CRYSTAL: granulated table sugar.

TABASCO SAUCE: made with vinegar, hot red peppers and salt. Use sparingly.

TACO SAUCE: found in supermarkets among Mexican ingredients.

TERIYAKI SAUCE: based on the lighter Japanese soy sauce; contains sugar, spices and vinegar.

TOMATO:
TOMATO PUREE: canned, pureed tomatoes (not tomato paste). Use fresh, peeled, pureed tomatoes, if preferred.
TOMATO SAUCE: tomato ketchup.
TOMATO SUPREME: a canned product consisting of tomatoes, onions, celery, peppers and seasonings.

TOMATOES, SUN-DRIED: are dried tomatoes sometimes bottled in oil.

TURMERIC: a member of the ginger family, its root is ground and dried, giving the rich yellow powder which gives curry its characteristic colour; it is not hot in flavour; use in small quantities.

VINEGAR: we used both white and brown (malt) vinegar in this book.
BALSAMIC: originated in the province of Modena, Italy. Regional wine is specially processed then aged in antique wooden casks to give pungent flavour.

WASABI: powdered green horseradish used in Japanese cooking. Substitute hot mustard powder or fresh, grated horseradish. It is usually sold in cans and mixed to a paste with cold water.

WATER CHESTNUTS: small white crisp bulbs with a brown skin. Canned water chestnuts are peeled and will keep for about 1 month, covered, in refrigerator.

WATER CRACKERS: savoury crackers.

WITLOF: chicory or Belgian endive.

WONTON WRAPPERS: are thin squares or rounds of fresh noodle dough. Cover with a damp cloth to prevent drying out while using.

WORCESTERSHIRE SAUCE: is a spicy sauce used mainly on red meat.

YEAST: 7g dry yeast (2 level metric teaspoons) is equal to 15g fresh compressed yeast.

ZUCCHINI: courgette.

Cup and Spoon Measurements

To ensure accuracy in your recipes use the standard metric measuring equipment approved by Standards Australia:
(a) 250 millilitre cup for measuring liquids. A litre jug *(capacity 4 cups)* is also available.
(b) a graduated set of four cups – measuring 1 cup, half, third and quarter cup – for items such as flour, sugar, etc. When measuring in these fractional cups, level off at the brim.
(c) a graduated set of four spoons: tablespoon *(20 millilitre liquid capacity)*, teaspoon *(5 millilitre)*, half and quarter teaspoons. The Australian, British and American teaspoon each has 5ml capacity.

Approximate cup and spoon conversion chart

Australian	American & British
1 cup	1¼ cups
¾ cup	1 cup
⅔ cup	¾ cup
½ cup	⅔ cup
⅓ cup	½ cup
¼ cup	⅓ cup
2 tablespoons	¼ cup
1 tablespoon	3 teaspoons

All spoon measurements are level.

Note: NZ, USA and UK all use 15ml tablespoons.

We have used large eggs with an average weight of 61g each in all recipes.

Oven Temperatures

Electric	C°	F°
Very slow	120	250
Slow	150	300
Moderately slow	160-180	325-350
Moderate	180-200	375-400
Moderately hot	210-230	425-450
Hot	240-250	475-500
Very hot	260	525-550
Gas		
Very slow	120	250
Slow	150	300
Moderately slow	160	325
Moderate	180	350
Moderately hot	190	375
Hot	200	400
Very hot	230	450

Index